ARCHITECTURAL PRESS LEGAL GUIDES

PROFESSIONAL LIABILITY

RAY CECIL

Cartoons by Louis Hellman

First published in 1984 by the Architectural Press Ltd, 9 Queen Anne's Gate, London SW1H 9BY

British Library Cataloguing in Publication Data

Cecil, Raymond
    Professional liability.—(Architectural Press legal guides)
    1. Architects—Malpractice—England
    2. Negligence—England
    I. Title
    344.2'063'2   KD2978

    ISBN 0–85139–956–8

Thanks are due to RIBA Publications Ltd for permission to reproduce from *Architects appointment*.

Designed by Roland Schenk

Typeset by Phoenix Photosetting, Chatham in 10/12pt Baskerville
Printed in Great Britain by
Biddles Ltd, Guildford, Surrey

CONTENTS

Acknowledgements

There are many references in this book to actual cases and happenings of which I have become aware. My appreciation is due to those set-upon members of my profession who have been willing to discuss their liability problems with me. It is due also to those members of the legal profession and insurance industry who have so often given me advice on specific topics.

My thanks also to my partners for their forbearance and to my wife, who bore the brunt of my reclusiveness.

Finally, my thanks to Tina, without whom this book would never have been typed—and re-typed—and amended and—

R.J.C.

There is probably no topic that causes an architect more concern than his professional liability. It was not always so, and it is because of the changing nature of the liability burden that this book has come about.

The book has been rather longer in the writing than I foresaw when I embarked on it. Significant changes in the law have occurred, even since I commenced, and others may happen before publication. No book on liability is ever up to date and yet 'plus ça change, plus c'est la même chose'. If you don't believe me, read The honeywood file,* written 60 years ago.

It would be pleasant to think that no architect was ever negligent, or that if he was, he had brought his troubles on himself. Most architects would profess that they themselves do not practise recklessly or negligently, but that unfortunately may be no more than their own honest opinion. It may not be the opinion held by a member of the public, an 'independent' expert, or a learned member of the judiciary.

Primarily, this book is written for architects, to advise, guide, and horribly warn them. But it also has a wider purpose, because the full impact of the liability burden is in its social cost. If architects cannot practise their profession free from the fears engendered by the wilder extravagances of the liability laws, then society pays an unseen bill. It is society that is denied the benefit of architects' expensively acquired and unique skills. And it is society that is deprived of the benefits of advancing technology.

My hope is that by demonstrating the practical effect of the law, the full enormity of the current situation will become evident to those who have more influence than architects alone to effect a change. So I make no apologies for the polemics in which I indulge here and there. Nor do I apologise for the absence of detailed case references—there are others more qualified than I to write them up, and very boring reading they make.

I should make it clear here, lest it should not be clear enough in the text, that I have written this book as an architect in practice, and that I am not an expert in either law or insurance matters. Indeed, the ground rules of both those topics seem to change with the weather, and their application depends on the minutiae and nuances of each particular case. So if you have a problem you will always need to seek specific advice.

Here is the situation. Here also are some very inadequate ways of dealing with it. Finally, here is a road down which we should travel if we are to find a real solution and the ability once again to practise our profession free from fear.

Raymond Cecil—1984

---

* Now available again as a boxed set comprising The honeywood file *and* The honeywood settlement, *published by Architectural Press, London, 1983.*

1: AN OUTLINE OF THE LAW

1.1 The law in a nutshell

I am not a lawyer, and until quite recently, my contact with lawyers and the judiciary was limited to those occasional brushes commonly experienced by all members of the public—the odd traffic offence, house purchase, and the occasional debt-chasing exercise. In the last few years, however, partly as a result of claims made against my own firm and partly because of my involvement at the RIBA in matters affecting the liability of architects, my exposure to the vagaries and iniquities of the law of liability has probably been greater than that of most practising architects. That by no means makes me an expert on the subject, on which very good books have been written, generally to be out of date even before publication. The law on liability is complex, full of uncertainties, and in a constant state of change. In this chapter, I do no more than set out in plain language the basic principles upon which the law appears to be based. This is to set the scene and the context within which I will attempt to give some guidance on how best to practise our profession with a modicum of safety, while still providing for our clients the standard of professional service which they and the public are entitled to expect from members of a venerable and learned professional institute.

1.1.1 The basis of liability

It is a precept of English law that if one man suffers loss or damage through the negligent act of another, then his remedy is in damages at law: unarguable, you might say, and right, reasonable, and just to boot.

It is another precept that if a man holds himself out to be an expert, the standards to be applied to his conduct in assessing his negligence will be more stringent than those applied to a layman. Reasonable enough, although you may question the definition of an expert.

It is no part of English law that the sins of the fathers shall be visited upon the children, even unto the third and fourth generation. Indeed, the reverse is true, and English law is full of legal amnesties such as the bankruptcy laws and the Limitation Acts. So how have architects found themselves carrying the burden of their 'sins' beyond the grave?

Accrual of cause and limitation receive a detailed treatment in 1.3, but for architects the problem of liability unlimited in time arises from a very simple piece of logic. A right to compensation arises from the suffering of loss, damage, or injury, caused by the negligent act of a person who owes the injured party a duty of care. No claim can be made until the injury has been suffered. In a case of loss, damage, or injury arising from building defects, this may not occur for many years after the negligent act that caused them. It is then that a claim may arise and time, as defined in the Limitation Acts, begin to run.

3

Many years after the negligent act

1.1.2 Liability in contract or tort
There are two principal ways in which one man can become liable to another
for damages: by breach of contract, or through the commission of a tort—that
is, the neglect of his common–law duty of care for the wellbeing of those other
people who might suffer as a result of his actions. It follows that one can be
guilty of a breach of contract only if there is a contractual relationship with
another party. Architects can commit breaches of contract with their clients,
but they owe no contractual duty, usually, to any of the other parties in the
building process. (There are exceptions to this rule which will be dealt with
below.) All architects must be aware of their contractual duties to their clients,
but because of the way in which the law has moved, claims against architects
are increasingly being mounted in tort, relating to the common-law duty
of care.

Until very recently indeed, there was a difference between one's liability in contract and one's liability in tort. A breach of contract could render one liable for
all the losses which might reasonably be expected to result from the breach. Not
only could an aggrieved client sue for the cost of rebuilding his collapsed building, he could also collect all his consequential losses. Suing under the common
law of tort, he could recover only his direct losses. That principle was breached
by the recent House of Lords decision in the case of *Junior Books* v *Veitchi*,
when it was held that a claimant in a case based on delict (the Scottish equivalent of negligence) had a right to recover his economic loss as well as the direct
cost of making good the physical damage his building had suffered.

So liability is unlimited in time, unlimited in scope, and very definitely unlimited in amount. It is possible (subject to the unfair contracts legislation)
to limit all three in contract and in tort with your client, but it is completely
impossible to limit in any way your common–law liabilities to third parties.
To make matters just that little bit worse, the law has also decided in recent
years that you can be sued in tort by somebody with whom you have a contractual relationship. So your contractual limitations may avail you little in
any event.

The final back-breaking straw is the Civil Liabilities (Contribution) Act. Anybody who is sued may join into the case further parties, and the judge will
decide the proportion of blame attributable to each. Inevitably, anybody sued
in respect of a defective building will join in the 'leader of the building team'
and, since *Anns* v *Merton*, the local authority is also a prime target.

However, in cases based on tort, although the percentage of blame that attaches
to each of the conjoined defendants may be adjudicated, the claimant may
look to any one of them for the whole of his loss. It is up to the unfortunate
target to recover his contributions from the other parties. If the other parties
have no resources, one defendant among many may have to pick up the whole
bill, even though his share of the blame was no more than 20 per cent or 10 per
cent, or, as in one case reported to me, a nominal 1 per cent.

1.1.3 The liability of local authorities
It should be noted, however, that the liability of local authorities is based on
their statutory duties to safeguard public health and safety, and in order to

succeed in a claim against a local authority, it is necessary to establish that there is imminent danger to the health and safety of the claimant. The imminence of the danger to health can, on occasion, be judicially fictionalised, as in the case concerning a house constructed not too close to a cliff edge, where the owner awoke one morning to discover that the cliff edge was appreciably nearer his house than it had been the night before. Although there was no imminent danger of the house being re-sited on the foreshore, nevertheless the courts found there was an imminent danger to health because of the effect of this happenstance on the nervous well-being of the owner's wife! However, in a recent case of foundation failure, where the local authority had been joined in, it was dismissed from the case because the degree of cracking in the walls of the house was comparatively minor, and capable of being made good. Admittedly the owner had suffered a severe economic loss, in that the house had to be underpinned, but there was no 'imminent danger to the health and safety' of anybody.

1.1.4 The climate of public opinion

English common law, the envy and example of a large proportion of the world, is a moving concept. It is based on precedent and judicial decisions which have been confirmed in the court of appeal, and sometimes (quite often, in fact) confirmed or reversed by the House of Lords. Its flexibility enables it to adjust to a changing climate of opinion, and some appeal judges (of whom the last Master of the Rolls, Lord Denning, is certainly the best known) at times have even anticipated the changing climate with their decisions.

We live in a time of changes, and one of the most noticeable is the increasing emphasis on the protection of the individual. As society grows more complex, it is acknowledged that the individual is less competent to safeguard his own health, safety, goods, chattels, and wealth. A vast body of legislation and procedure has evolved to protect the individual from himself (seat belts, crash helmets), from those with whom he has contractual dealings (employee protection, hire-purchase and credit laws), from the world at large (motor insurance, the general right to damages), and from the fates (criminal injuries compensation, disaster funds). This has given rise to the belief now widely held that if a citizen suffers a loss or damage that is not clearly and incontrovertibly his own fault (and sometimes when it is), then somebody else shall compensate him. The only problem sometimes is to find a potential compensator who is both extant and possessed of the means to compensate. Where damage arising from buildings is concerned, the architect, leader of the building team, is an evident and available target.

We are not going to change the climate of public opinion, so if we are to survive to practise our profession as we know it, we are clearly going to have to change the law.

From his books, it is clear that Lord Denning at times made his apparently aberrant judgements in order to create public debate and was not always disappointed to see his rulings reversed. In the meantime, the topic had been aired and change would follow. It is quite likely that the law on latent defects will change again as a result of this process, but whether it will do so sufficiently to bring comfort to our profession is another thing.

1.2 The law of tort

When an architect undertakes a professional commitment, he enters into a
contract. (Here I am referring not only to the contract between client and consultant, but also to such commitments as contracts of employment and all those
other less clear arrangements between architect and architect, such as 'self-
employment', agency work, ghosting, and subcontracting.) He has a contractual
duty to exercise his professional skill competently and with care in his client's
interest. If he has inadequate skill or fails to exercise his skills with due diligence
and care, thereby damaging his client's interest, then he will be in breach of
contract. The ways in which an architect may breach his contract would make a
very long list, although no architect has ever been sued by his client for designing an ugly building!

Mostly, architects understand their contractual liabilities and, mostly, they
comply with them. Indeed, they have every incentive to comply with them, if
only to ensure the continuation of a relationship which is hard to come by. The
dread of all professional men is that they may inadvertently cause their client
damage. This is something that can happen even in the best regulated practices,
and recognising this, the prudent architect will insure against the contingency
so that he will be in a position to make good his client's loss.

1.2.1 Damage to remote third parties

But an architect's liability extends far beyond his contractual duties to his client
or employer. In a general sense, this wider liability is even written into the
RIBA's Code of Conduct, which refers to the architect's responsibilities to
'those who will use and enjoy his buildings'.

This wider liability is covered by the common law of tort. If a passer–by is
struck by a piece of falling masonry and suffers injury or worse, he (or his
dependents) will look for compensation to the owner of the building in the first
instance. The claim will be based on the building owner's common–law duty
of care to maintain his building in a safe condition. If the masonry fell because
the builder had failed to provide the proper fixings, the builder in his turn might
be sued, either by the building owner (for breach of contract) or by the injured
party for a breach of his common–law duty of care. In this event, the architect
would probably be sued also—why not?—for a breach of his duty of care in
'supervision'. If, on investigation, it appeared that the builder had correctly
installed the fixings but that the fixings themselves were inadequate, we would
have a design fault, and the architect might be sued. He would have been in
breach of his duty of care to the world at large, and it would avail him little to
plead that the client's budget was too small to permit the inclusion of sufficient
fixings. His common–law duty of care overrides his contractual duty to his
client to get the job out within budget.

The instance of the falling masonry, in itself a clear case of damage suffered by a
third party from building failure, illustrates many of the problems faced by the
architect's profession. Suppose the stone fell off the building 20 years after
completion, that the original client company no longer existed, and that the new
building owner had let the space on a full repairing lease, which he had failed to
enforce. The architect, approaching retirement, had destroyed or lost the

original documents, and a small spate of similar failures had disclosed that, in a given set of circumstances, the techniques adopted on this particular building would lead to this type of failure. There was evidence to show that, at the date the building was designed, some architects were already aware of the possibility and adopted different techniques.

There are many ways in which architects may damage third parties, some rather less obvious than in the case of the falling masonry. The architect's involvement with the building process is ubiquitous and diffuse. There is no part of the process in which the architect is not involved in some manner, from initial feasibility right through the design and construction processes to final handover and beyond.

'Beyond' is very important, because architects are increasingly providing maintenance manuals with their buildings, and if defective maintenance instructions lead to failure, loss, or damage, an architect may well find himself sued by a subsequent owner, who in law is deemed entitled to rely upon the professional advice in the manual.

1.2.2 Damage to known third parties

Liability to third parties can be seemingly remote, or it can be immediate. Of immediate concern are the architect's liabilities to third parties in his administration of the building contract. These concerns fall into two main categories—liability to contractors, and liability to parties in a contractual relationship with the client.

If, through his actions, an architect causes loss or damage to a contractor, the contractor will usually have a choice of two remedies. He may claim against the employer whose agent the architect is. This is the most usual remedy, but it will not help the architect, because the employer will then simply look to his architect for reimbursement. More rarely, but with increasing frequency, a builder may look directly to the architect if he suffers loss or damage as a result of the architect's negligent or improper actions. The architect's functions in respect of the standard contract include a duty to interpret it fairly, and this can be a veritable minefield, particularly when the employer takes the narrow view that the architect is being paid by him and accordingly should take his—the employer's—side in disputed matters.

The architect is also at risk in relation to the builder in dealing with the internecine strife between contractor and subcontractors. The issue or withholding of certificates of delay can involve either party in very heavy financial loss. The issues and contractual details may be extremely complex and, if a lot of money is involved, it is worth seeking legal advice before making a decision. If your client won't meet the bill, ask the warring parties to. If they won't pay, it may well be worth your while to foot the bill yourself.

Finally, a topic dealt with more fully in 2.10, the architect's duty to third parties in respect of certificates of completion. It is common practice in conveyancing and leasing to designate one or other of the architect's certificates as the trigger to cause other events to run—for rent to be payable, for freeholds to change ownership, for liabilities to be undertaken, and so on. The architect may or may not have specific knowledge of these arrangements, but they are so common that the courts will deem the architect to be able reasonably to expect that they exist. A duty of care to contracting third parties must be recognised when you issue certificates.

1.3 Accrual of cause and limitation

Fathers sometimes play cricket with their small sons in the back garden. If they are prudent, they will play with a soft ball or erect a high fence around the garden. If they play with a hard ball without a protective fence, then they must be very careful indeed how and where they hit the ball.

If a rush of blood to the head is followed by a Botham-style six-hit, damage to a third party is likely to follow. If the ball goes through a window, that is damage to property, and if it hits the neighbour's head, that is personal injury. If the ball smashes a greenhouse and the neighbour's prize orchids die, then there will also be consequential loss.

A domestic mishap of this nature will usually be resolved by an apology and an offer to pay for the damage—but neighbours are not always neighbourly and may not even be on speaking terms. For that matter, it may not be the first time this particular negligent act has resulted in loss or damage. What are the neighbour's legal rights? His remedy lies in the law of tort, the tort in this case being the negligence of his cricketing neighbour. And his rights begin to run as soon as he suffers the damage. It is suffering the damage that gives rise to what is known as 'accrual of cause', not, you note, the negligent act itself—although in the case of the carelessly smitten cricket ball, the negligent act and accrual of cause are to all intents and purposes contemporaneous.

The damaged party is not required instantly to launch himself into litigation. He can consider the situation, he can take advice, he can wait to see whether the damage is greater than he first thought, and he can enter into a long wrangling correspondence exchanging insults and threats, as is not uncommon between unfriendly neighbours. He may even decide to do nothing, holding the threat of action as a sort of security against his neighbour's future behaviour, rather like a suspended sentence in the criminal courts. So the careless cricketer may have his carelessness hanging over his head for a long while—but not for ever. The law, through the Statute of Limitations, recognises (with certain exceptions, of which one is the principal reason for this book) that no man should remain in jeopardy for ever. So the injured neighbour has six years from the date of the accrual of cause in which to commence legal proceedings. If he is suing in respect of personal injury, then the time limit is three years.

Because of the contemporaneous nature of the negligent act and accrual of cause in most tortious actions, the belief was current until about 15 years ago that a man could not be sued more than six years after the action that caused the damage. This followed closely the position in cases of breach of contract, where a case could not be brought more than six years after the breach of the contract, or 12 years if the contract was under seal. In fact, the belief is still current, if one may judge from the standard professional indemnity proposal form, which even today poses a question about contracts under seal—as if it made any difference.

To extend the analogy a little: suppose the ball from the neighbour's garden does not, as is usual with rising objects, immediately descend to earth but lodges instead in a rainwater outlet, unrecovered and unseen. Not until there is a heavy downpour may damage occur, causing a flood in the best bedroom, ruining carpets, bedding, and curtains. The damage flows directly, but not immediately, from the negligent act—it is latent damage. It is the flood damage that is the cause of action, and it is the date of the flood that triggers off the limitation period. Even if the neighbour was on holiday when the flood occurred and knew nothing of it until his return, it is still the date of the flood itself that is significant. That is the meaning of the judgement in *Pirelli* v *Oscar Faber*, overturning the previous ruling that the accrual of cause was when the claimant might with reasonable diligence have discovered he had been damaged.

1.3.1 Erosion of the six-year rule
The first wedge driven between a defendant and the protection afforded by the Statute of Limitations was a building case featuring defective foundations. The damage did not reveal itself until long after the expiration of six years from the date of practical completion. The builder pleaded that the case was 'time-barred'. On a preliminary hearing of that issue, the courts found that, even though there had been no fraudulent concealment, the breach of contract could not have been detected by normal inspection, either while the work was being done, or at practical completion. Detection was delayed until the defective foundations actually failed and the damage revealed itself above ground.

It is no mere coincidence that that was a building case, because buildings, by their very nature, can conceal defects for a very long time, but the damage, when it reveals itself, can be substantial indeed in money terms. But don't think only the construction industry is subject to latent defects. Lawyers, in particular, can cause damage that does not evince itself for many years. A defectively drawn will can be stored unseen in a deed box for 30 years, and only on the demise of the testator may a beneficiary discover that he has been disinherited through the lawyer's negligence. Similar problems can arise in the conveyancing of property, the failure to register options, or charges on property, and so on.

A whole string of cases in recent years has eroded the concept of the six-year rule in a number of ways. *Anns* v *Merton*, so often quoted as the cause of our problems, did not involve architects or the design of buildings at all. It was primarily about the duties of local authorities and their inspectors in administering the Building Regulations, and whether they had a direct responsibility to future occupants of the building. *Anns* v *Merton* was not even out of time, and it was only a judicial aside in the judgement that set off the new conception of accrual of cause. The cause of the damage may well have been a negligent act, but the cause of action arises only when—?
Well, when does it arise?

Three years ago, the Lord Chancellor's Law Reform Committee (LRC) set up a subcommittee to look into that very subject. In an extremely lengthy consultative document, the sub-committee posited that perhaps the law as it was being operated was not fulfilling the ends of justice, and that there was a need to

balance the interests of both claimant and defendant, together with the public
interest. The document, in a blinding glimpse of the obvious, averred that a
man should not be penalised because he did not initiate proceedings until he
knew that he had suffered damage. It also acknowledged the intolerable burden
this placed on potential defendants, who might never be free from the threat of
legal pursuit arising from some action almost lost in the mists of time.

The consultative document directed attention to accrual of cause and suggested
three definitions: when the negligent act was committed; when the damaged
party suffered the loss; and when the damage was discovered or could reasonably have been expected to be discovered.

Leaving to one side for the moment the question whether any of these
definitions might serve the ends of justice and society, they were proposed
before the House of Lords delivered its judgement in *Pirelli* v *Oscar Faber*,
when their lordships discovered that the law as it currently stood required yet
another definition: the date when the damage occurred! It did not escape them
that the damage in that case took place at the top of a 160 ft high chimney and
that nobody could reasonably have been expected to discover it. They acknowledged that the law was unsatisfactory, but they considered that their task was
merely to interpret the law—it was for Parliament to change it.

As Lord Scarman, who pronounced these strictures, is also chairman of the Law
Reform Committee, there is an irony in the situation—but at the time of writing
there are no signs of urgent endeavour from the Lord Chancellor's office.
Whatever emerges from the Law Reform Committee, perhaps finally to be
enacted by Parliament, I fear that it will do little to ease the uncertainties of
the present situation. The problems of latent defects in construction will, in my
view, not be solved in the context of generic legislation. It is the generic nature
of our common law that is at the root of our problems with time limitation. To
attempt to apply the same law to a window broken by a carelessly hit ball, to the
Thalidomide disaster, and to the products of the building industry may be
worthy. It is not very good sense. Special cases need special law, and construction—like the development, manufacture, and distribution of drugs—needs
special law.

1.3.2 *The need for certainty*

I deal elsewhere with the difficulties faced by a damaged party in establishing
blame in building-failure cases and the burden that places on the industry and
society. What is perhaps of greatest moment is that legal rights are illusory if
there is no certainty that compensation can actually be obtained from the
offending party. To some extent this is true throughout our legal system, but in
construction, because of the sums and time-scale involved, uncertainty is probably the rule rather than the exception. Statistics on building failures are hard
to come by and notoriously unreliable. We do know, however, that only a very
small proportion of claims ever come to trial. *Eames* v *North London Estates
& Others* hit the headlines a few years ago and is one of the leading cases on
latent defects for a number of reasons. But the real interest of the case was in the
banner headline of a construction weekly: ' "I'LL GO BANKRUPT", SAYS
ARCHITECT'. The architect concerned had no insurance and had perforce

to conduct his own defence in the case. Whether he would have fared better with professional representation is a moot point. In effect, he was dragged along by the other defendants, held to be liable for between 35 per cent and 40 per cent of the damage, and faced a bill of £150,000

In the event, he was not made bankrupt, and the claimants accepted a very much smaller sum in discharge of his share. Whether they got all or part of the shortfall from the other defendants, who included the local authority, I do not know. If the local authority had not been a defendant and the claimants had had to seek their remedy against other defendants in the same position as the architect, they would still be whistling for their legal rights. And disappearing or insubstantial defendants are by no means rare.

How can certainty be created? As the law stands, if there is to be certainty of compensation, it is necessary for at least one of the liable parties still to exist at the time a claim is settled or adjudicated, and that he shall have available funds sufficient to match the damage. The only cases in which this is assured at present are those in which one of the liable parties can be shown to be a perpetual body, such as a local authority. One is compelled towards the view that the present fashion for joining in local authorities is largely caused by this consideration, and that it is likely to become the rule. It takes only a small stretch of imagination to envisage the local authorities picking up the whole tab for building defects, if the law is allowed to develop on these lines. It is not for me to suggest that this is one of the reasons why the Government is so anxious to privatise the building control service, but by now the thought must have crossed the bureaucratic mind, even if it is not part of the ministerial intention. Indeed, it is recognised that the problems of perpetual and un-limited liability constitute a major impediment to the creation of a private certification service.

Some might think it no bad thing that the local authorities should bear the full responsibility for defective buildings constructed within their bailiwicks. But the local authority is you, me, and the man on the Clapham omnibus, and mature consideration quickly reveals the injustice of that line of thought. It is rather like having the police reimburse you when a burglar steals the family jewels.

There is no way in which the existence of the parties to a building's creation can be guaranteed at any time after completion. Companies liquidate or are 're-organised', people die or remove themselves from the jurisdiction of the courts. Even if they exist, there can be no guarantee that the parties will be in a position to meet any settlement. They may be insured, but there can be no guarantee that the insurance will be adequate. Increasingly, there are cases where the size of claims and settlements far exceeds the limits of indemnity, and that is not necessarily because the sum insured was unreasonably or recklessly low. Indemnity limits in professional indemnity policies are those set in the year a claim is notified. With settlement often taking five or more years, inflation at even modest rates can render seemingly adequate indemnity limits far too small.

1.3.3 The creation of certainty

There is in fact only one way in which a reasonable degree of certainty can be

created, and that is by way of an insurance policy written for the benefit of the
building owner. Then, if a defect arises, the building owner has a claim on the
policy and is immediately put into funds to enable him to effect repairs. How
that policy might be written, and who might pay for it, is dealt with elsewhere,
but the principle is clear, and it meets one of the biggest objections to the
present system—the time it takes for the damaged party to obtain his compensation, time during which the defect may seriously worsen and the cost of
the remedy will inevitably increase.

A well-publicised comment by Owen Luder is that even today the descendants
of Wren could be sued for a defect in St Paul's. That may be a little far–
fetched, but I am aware of one case where an architect is defending himself in
respect of a bungalow which he designed (town planning and building regulations only) for a friend in 1952.

In a limited sense, the house builder's guarantee scheme already serves the
domestic market. The guarantee is backed by insurance, and the NHBC has a
wide enough spread of risk to make underwriting comparatively simple. The
insurers may have rights of redress against the parties causing the defect, but
at least the interest of the house owner is assured. But even the NHBC
guarantee is time-limited. As things stand at present, once the guarantee period
has expired, a damaged owner has, at least in theory, some recourse directly to
the original designers and builders if they still exist.

In its submission to the LRC sub-committee on latent defects, the RIBA
proposed that in respect of building defects, the latest date for accrual of cause
should be the date of practical completion of a building, and that thereafter the
six-year rule of the Statute of Limitations should run. It further recommended
that, in any case, there should be a long-stop of 10 years after a building
designer had been involved with a project. This was to protect the architect who
performs a partial service and may have no part in the construction process,
which may not even commence for a number of years. There may be debate
about whether six years from completion is long enough, but the merit of the
proposal is the certainty it would create for the building owner. He would
know that after six years he had to accept responsibility for his building, and
this was a matter which he could deal with at his discretion and by means of
insurance.

All the other organisations concerned with construction made similar submis-
sions, and while each one opted for a different period of liability, and there were
differences on the definition of accrual of cause, there was absolute unanimity
that there should be a statutory time limit.

1.4 The law of contribution

A recent factor that has considerably bedevilled cases concerned with building
defects is the Civil Liabilities (Contribution) Act 1976. Ironically, the law was
introduced in order to simplify a process which had become increasingly complex over the years. Previously, a damaged party could sue one or more parties
whom he thought to be responsible. If the defendant thought that responsibility
could in whole or in part be attributed to somebody else who owed him a
duty, or who owed a duty in tort to the plaintiff, then the defendant could issue

a separate writ against that person. The Civil Liabilities (Contribution) Act now enables a defendant to join in for contribution, not only those parties who owe him a duty, but also parties who owe a duty to the original claimant. The court then has the power to allocate the proportion of blame attributable to each of the defending parties.

In an unhappy case referred to later in this book, the architect concerned is retired, extremely elderly, and in poor health. The claimants, on being made aware of the circumstances, offered not to proceed against the architect, but they pointed out that if the builders, who were also being sued, joined in the architect for contribution, they would be able to do nothing about it.

There is a particularly nasty quirk in the Civil Liabilities (Contribution) Act which relates to limitation. The accrual of cause in a contribution action is the award of damages against a defendant in the principal case. An action for contribution can be commenced within two years of accrual of cause. What this means is that, while a direct liability for building defects extends only to eternity, one's liability for contribution extends to eternity plus two years, which may aid the recruiting figures for the Campaign for Nuclear Disarmament but certainly does little to ensure a peaceful night's rest for anybody engaged in the building industry.

In practice, what happens is that a party who has suffered damage by a defect in a building may issue his claim against the most obviously responsible parties. Commonly, a writ will be issued against the builder (if he still exists), the architect, perhaps the local authority, and maybe the engineer. Each of those defendants will, at some stage, search around to see who else might be brought in to share the burden. Often this may not become apparent until some considerable time into the proceedings, and they have been served with 'further and better particulars' and/or a Scott schedule, and the complaints are set out in detail. At this stage, any number of other defendants can be brought in for contribution in respect of individual matters which might be in dispute. I have heard of one case in which the total number of defendants reached 25, and while that may be exceptional, cases with 10 or more defendants are becoming increasingly common.

The final injustice of the law on contribution is that while the judge in the case may allocate the various percentages of blame attributable to each of the defendants, the claimant can levy his damages against any one of them. and it is up to that defendant to obtain his reimbursement from the other contributors. If any of these contributors is without financial resources, or with inadequate resources, then the defendant against whom the damages have been levied will have to put it down to dame fortune, the rub of the green, or just damned bad luck!

1.4.1 The duck-shoot

Cases concerned with defects in buildings increasingly are taking on the character of a duck-shoot. It is an appropriate term, and the analogy is clear—particularly if one considers the normal claim for damages to be in the nature of a deerstalking expedition.

The complexity of the building process is such that it is seldom, if ever, possible

The duck-shoot

to point the finger of blame unerringly at a single culprit. To be fair to the claimant, who can be foiled in so many ways by the vagaries of the law and the effluxion of time, the only sensible advice he can be given by his lawyers is to use a wide-bore gun and well spread shot. In that way, his chances of success must be enhanced, and if he can include a local authority, with perpetual existence and a bottomless purse, his chances of actually being paid any damages he may be awarded must be very good indeed. The fashion for joining in local authorities must be a very worrying one for our legislators to contemplate, and this may more than anything else lead to a change in the law sooner than we might otherwise have hoped.

The duck-shoot has quite dramatically altered the process involved in the settling of building-defects claims. Where there is a single claimant and a single defendant, it may be a comparatively simple matter, after an initial ritual dance, to sit down across a table and arrive at some sort of satisfactory settlement. The duck-shoot has altered all that. Quite apart from the difficulty of finding a table large enough for the various parties to sit down around, each party is concerned to defend himself not only against the claimant, but also against the allegations and counterclaims of all the other defendants. Each party mounts his claim and allegations and defences against all the other parties, and brings to his aid and assistance the evidence of independent experts in each and every area of dispute. Time goes on, papers and documents and drawings proliferate exponentially, and one hears of cases where the amount of documentation is eventually such that pantechnicons have to be hired to transport them all to court.

I am no luddite, but I certainly yearn for a return to the days before xerography and the instant copier. I am sure it is no mere fancy on my part that without the facility for instant spew, building cases would revert to the occasional deer stalk, the analogy I mentioned earlier.

Because of the difficulty of achieving settlement with the many parties involved in a duck-shoot, even those who would be disposed to settle are dragged along in a welter of paper, the attending of conferences, the reading of documents, because if they sit back, their own case is likely to be severely prejudiced. Nobody is prepared to show weakness while this game of bluff and counter-bluff goes on, and it is not until there is a serious possibility of a case going to trial that any real effort is made at settlement. It is only when arrangements are being made to set a date for a hearing that the full horror of the situation seems to dawn on anybody, because the first question that is asked is, 'How long is the case likely to last?' and a quick calculation will precipitate the answer: six weeks—six months—a year or more. Even finding a place large enough to accommodate the leading counsel, junior counsel, solicitors, experts, and defendants may present a problem, and for some of the participants at least, the amount of time they will actually have to spend in the courtroom and away from their other business is a matter of major concern. Thus it is that many duck-shoots are settled 'on the steps of the court' by methods more reminiscent of a western poker game than of the blindfolded lady with a sword in her hand.

1.4.2 The burden of costs

All of this makes handsome pickings for the lawyers and the experts, who tend to come expensive—£100 per hour for a specialist solicitor is by no means uncommon. For the defendants, the cost in time, worry, and out–of–pocket expenses may be a burden they can ill afford. Even the claimant is probably worse off because of the passage of time since he sustained his loss, and because no litigant—even one who wins on every point—ever recovers the full extent of his costs.

It would be a comfort to think that the iniquity, inequity, and wastefulness of this process would have dawned on those who have the power to change it. The reverse is true. Since *Anns* v *Merton*, it has become common practice to join the local authority in as a party to building-failure cases, and the latest proposals for privatising the building control process presume the liability of independent certifiers.

If the reader should believe that I am exaggerating to make my point, I would quote just one case involving a defective air-conditioning installation, where the tenant of the building sued the owners, and separately sued the architects, the consultants, the main contractor, the sub-contractor, and an equipment supplier. The building owner, not to be outdone, sued all the same parties and, for good measure, the senior partner of the architects and the senior partner of the consultants.

As an illustration of the way that costs can exceed the damage, consider the case of a house designed by an architect for a fee of £1,250. By the time the case was adjudicated, the rebuilding cost was £88,000 (original cost £26,000) and the legal costs on both sides exceeded £160,000.

That is an illustration of the costs involved in what was a comparatively small case. I recently learned of a case concerning damages claimed in a sum of several million pounds. With some 25 defendants involved, it was estimated that combined costs had already exceeded £2 m, with neither settlement nor hearing yet within sight.

Perhaps the greater evil generated by the duck-shoot is the way in which it forces all parties into defensive attitudes. Nobody is particularly interested to find out just what has gone wrong to cause the damage—only to show that it was not his liability. Most particularly, the architect is driven into an invidious position. If a building exhibits a defect, the owner will generally contact the architect in the first instance, and the architect's initial reaction will be a desire to assist his client in identifying the cause and remedying it. He may even feel that his relationship with his client is so good that it will survive the discovery that the architect himself has not been blameless.

Two warnings. First, if the fault rests with the builder or subcontractor, for a certainty the architect will receive a 'third party notice', alleging defective design, or negligent supervision or site instructions, and in assisting his client he may well be digging his own grave. Second, he should always notify his insurers before doing *anything*. Failure to do so may result in their repudiating liability.

1.4.3 The paper war

I have already referred to some of the various documents which constitute the ammunition in any legal proceedings relating to building defects. While in no sense does this volume pretend to be a legal textbook, a few words about the various documents figuring in such litigation may be useful for those readers who have had the great good fortune not so far to have been involved.

1.4.3.1 Preliminary skirmishes

Most litigation is preceded by a certain amount of preliminary correspondence, the tone of which will usually indicate that the architect should notify his insurers of a possible claim. In advance of a formal claim, there will often be a request for the architect to accept responsibility for the damage, or for a sum of money, and so on. There may even be an offer to settle.

At this stage, correspondence will probably be clearly marked with the superscription 'without prejudice'. This term is so often used loosely and inappropriately that it is worth describing just what it means. It can best be paraphrased as follows: 'In this document, I am attempting to settle by compromise the dispute that exists between us. In making the statements or offers embodied in this letter, I do not depart from the legitimacy of my original claim (or defence). If we fail to agree, then this letter may not be used in any subsequent litigation to *prejudice* my claim (or defence)'.

Were it not for the device of the 'without prejudice' letter, pre-trial negotiations and settlements would be virtually impossible. If attempts at amicable settlement fail, then the following documentation will ensue.

1.4.3.2 Threat of writ

Usually a letter from a solicitor stating the intention to serve a writ and asking whether you or your solicitor will accept service. This is no more than a civility and an attempt to save time and trouble.

1.4.3.3. The Writ

A formal document issued by the court stating only the briefest facts of the nature of the claim. A claimant may take out a writ, and the date of the issue marks the commencement of the litigation for the purposes of the Limitation Acts. The defendant may not know that a writ has been taken out at this stage.

The claimant has one year in which to serve a writ after it has been issued.

1.4.3.4 Statement of claim

A writ, when served, will be accompanied by a statement of claim. This will set out in general terms the legal basis of the claim (i.e. breach of contract or tortious acts) and the nature of the damage for which the claimant is seeking compensation. Very often, there will be no indication of the monetary value of the claim.

1.4.3.5 Defence (and counterclaim)

Service of the writ together with the statement of claim requires an answer within a specified period. This answer usually takes the form of a blanket denial of all the allegations in the statement except the facts of the architect's appointment. It is often accompanied in the same document by a counterclaim.

1.4.3.6 Further and better particulars
The defence will either be accompanied or closely followed by a request for 'further and better particulars'. This is a means by which the defence puts pressure on the claimant to disclose all the facts he is relying on to support his claim. Where allegations of negligence have been made, the request for further and better particulars will ask specifically what it is that the architect has done or failed to do that constitutes negligence. The response will usually be accompanied by an expert witness's report.

1.4.3.7 The Scott schedule
Building cases being so complicated, a document has been devised to set out in an analysed form the various aspects of the claim. Set out in columns, each item in the claim will have recorded against it: the defective act; the effect of the defective act; the remedial action necessary; and the cost of the remedial action. If there is more than one defendant, the schedule will include separate columns for each of them, and all in all, it can become a most voluminous document.

It is with the service of the 'Scott schedule' that the defendant will discover the amount of money being claimed in respect of remedial work. Even now, however, he may still not know the amount claimed in respect of consequential losses.

1.4.3.8 Third party notices
It is often on examination of the Scott schedule that the defence will decide that other parties so far not involved may be held to have had some share in causing one or more of the defects resulting in damage. In order to join them into the case, the defendant serves on these other parties what are termed 'third party notices'. In essence, a third party notice is the equivalent of the writ and statement of claim served by the claimant on the original defendant. It locks the third parties into the main case. Third party notices will, in turn, precipitate an exchange of paper between the defendant and the third parties.

1.5 What is negligence?
I frame this heading in the form of a question, not to demonstrate my own erudition in answering it, but because the word means different things to different people. But an understanding of the judicial concept of negligence is crucial for architects.

Time was when a professional man adjudged guilty of negligence in the pursuit of his craft would have been disowned by his colleagues and quite possibly ruined in his career. The exercise of care in a professional sense was taken for granted, and those who departed from the highest standards were considered black sheep who could expect no sympathy from their fellows. The reaction of a professional accused of negligence would be to fight like fury to defend his good name.

But the judicial concept of negligence is a moving one, and practitioners have gradually come to realise that it may not carry quite the stigma it once did. The judiciary tends to follow public opinion and to dispense justice in line with the prevailing expectations and mores of the day. In an increasingly commercial and materialistic society, much of the respect—even awe—in which the professional man was once held has dissipated, and the client increasingly sees himself as a customer. How much the professions have themselves contributed to this situation is open to debate, as is the extent to which it has been brought about by the proliferation of professions and a general debasement of the word 'professional'.

Allied to this trend has been a weakening of the personal relationship which used to exist between a practitioner and his client. Increasingly clients are corporations 'with no body to be kicked nor soul to be damned', and often a practitioner will not even know the man who has the power to authorise his appointment or sanction proceedings in a claim. With claims from third parties, there is often no relationship at all between claimant and defendant. Claims are launched quite impersonally, merely as a way of obtaining compensation with no thought at all of the personalities involved. Indeed, in most cases, no personal hurt may be intended. Some years ago, I was invited to a meeting to be briefed on a major commission. I thought it proper to draw to the commissioning surveyor's attention the fact that his organisation had just served a writ on me in respect of a long-dead project. 'Oh,' he said, 'that's our legal and management departments. It doesn't affect this job at all'. But were they happy to commission an architect they were claiming had practised negligently? Of course they were, because they were quite confident that I did not practise negligently. And even if they won their case, their view would not alter. A finding of negligence no longer necessarily means that you are negligent, nor may there be any stigma attached to such a finding. Negligence today may be no more than a legal fiction devised by lawyers and supported or rebutted by experts with the benefit of hindsight.

My dictionary definitions of negligence are, 'a want of proper care or attention; habitual neglect; omission of duty, especially such care for the interests of others *as the law may require*' (my italics). You will note that all these definitions, except the last, are unquantified.

If, however, I were asked for a definition of the current judicial view of professional negligence, it would be, 'getting wrong that which another practitioner more often than not would get right'.

Current practice is for the claimants to prove negligence by means of expert evidence. This is why we have a situation where an architect may be adjudged to have been negligent when quite clearly he had exercised great care and dedication in his work. In court, what is examined is not the care and dedication of the architect–defendant, but the 'state of the art' in respect of the particular defect complained of.

A claimant's expert witness will be invited to express his opinion as to whether, in respect of the particular fault complained of, an average practitioner would have performed as the defendant had. He will be asked whether the knowledge of the average practitioner would have extended to the particular matter where the defendant is alleged to have been lacking. It takes but the barest understanding of the building process, and of the architect's ubiquitous and extensive role within it, to predict the expert's answer in most cases.

What the expert is being questioned about is not whether the defendant has exercised the skill and care of the average practitioner, but about the state of the art at the time the allegedly defective service was provided. There are a number of factors to be noted here.

First, we are talking about the state of the art among average practitioners. In effect, the expert, with the benefit of hindsight, is being asked whether 'the average practitioner' would have committed this particular fault—not, you observe, whether a specialist, or expert, or academic would have committed it. While, on the face of it, this is a fair question, it stands to reason that unless the fault is one commonly committed, the answer will always be to the detriment of the defendant.

Second, the expert is being asked to project his thoughts back to the state of the art at the time the fault was committed. Knowledge and methods of practice disseminate comparatively slowly in the construction industry, because of the timescale of the activity. It is all very well for the expert to aver that the average practitioner ought to have known something, or to have behaved in a particular way, several years earlier. There are usually no finite standards of comparison, so the outcome of any case may well depend solely on which side engages the most impressive expert.

Third, the experts will not usually be asked for an opinion as to whether the defendant was negligent. That is a decision for the court to make. As I said earlier, the courts tend to make their decisions accord with public sentiment and expectation. If the public sentiment is that the claimant, having suffered damage, deserves compensation, then the probability is that the court will see that he gets it. If that means distorting the commonsense meaning of negligence, then so be it.

It seems to me that the law concerning negligence is being abused and debased in order to comply with social views on product liability. The general body of consumer protection today ensures that, with most manufactured artefacts, the consumer has a right to compensation or replacement if the artefact fails to give satisfactory service. But the Trade Descriptions Acts, Sale of Goods Act, etc., do not cover the main products of the construction industry when they are procured through the conventional procedures. There is no Law of Absolute Product Liability, although the public's view is probably that it is entitled to the protection of such a law. Until either the law or the method of building procurement changes, we will continue to see the law relating to negligence distorted in order to serve the same purpose.

Given the changing state of the law, how can an architect best reduce his exposure to claims in negligence? It has to be accepted that his vulnerability is great in any event, that there is no sure protection, and that even immaculate performance provides no guarantee that claims will not be made, even though there appears to be a perfect defence.

In the following chapters, I examine the principal activities of an architect, indicate the areas of risk, and suggest ways in which the architect may reduce his exposure by understanding the nature of his liability and by organising his work and thought process in the light of that understanding.

2: THE MAIN AREAS OF RISK

2.1 Are architects negligent?

It is inevitable in a book of this nature that the general tenor will be defensive, with the implication that the law is all wrong and architects are all perfect. Only a fool or a rogue would attempt to maintain such a stance, and it has to be conceded that there are architects, as there are members of all trades, callings, and professions, who behave recklessly, negligently, carelessly, and/or incompetently, occasionally or constantly. Whenever the law on defects is discussed or the unreasonable liability of architects called into question, one is faced with the undeniable fact that a large proportion of building failures are due to matters which certainly ought to have been within the knowledge of the 'average practitioner'.

I will come back to this point, but first an apology for the vagueness of the terms 'a large proportion'. One of our problems in dealing with building defects is that we have little well-substantiated knowledge of the size of the problem or of the true causes of the failures. With embarrassing regularity, either the lay press or the technical journals will highlight a particular problem—a major building (New Scotland Yard or Great Ormond Street hospital), or a class of building ('£30 million to repair new hospitals', 'Council to demolish tower blocks') or a particular defect ('Thousands of houses affected by condensation')—but we seldom hear the end of those sagas, let alone the many that never reach the press at all. Settlements out of court are usually worded to be as uninformative as possible, and even reports of court cases dwell more on the legal niceties than on the technical faults.

This lack of hard information arises from the confidentiality of the relationship between insurers and insured. A vast body of information on building defects lies undisturbed in the files of the insurers, and even the RIBA has been unable to obtain any decent statistical information from the ABS insurance agency that arranges liability cover for over 60 per cent of the profession. The grounds on which the information has been refused has been 'commercial sensitivity', although recently some access has been granted to the files on a limited basis to see if any general or specific lessons could be drawn.

At the time of writing, the RIBA has launched its own information-gathering operation. For the first time, it has circularised every practice in the UK with a two-part questionnaire, the first dealing with the practice's insurance arrangements, and the second part, in much more detail, dealing with specific claims. The sceptics said that the profession would not respond, and that practitioners would keep their problems to themselves. Not so! A 40 per cent response has confounded the critics and overwhelmed the resources available for dealing with it. Some preliminary results are given in the appendix. They are already forming the basis for further action in preventing defects, in defending unreasonable claims, and in attempting to achieve changes in the law.

One fact that is becoming clear from the available information is that there is almost no limit to the ways in which an architect may be held to have damaged either his client or a third party by some act or omission in the pursuit of his profession. From his very first contact until long after completion of a building, the actions or omissions of an architect can have far-reaching and often disastrous effects. No list can be exhaustive, if only because construction is a changing world, but the section that follows is an attempt at highlighting those areas where an architect is most at risk.

2.2 Preliminary and basic services
In its publication *Architect's appointment*, the RIBA lists the various work stages by which the architect's work proceeds. That is therefore the pattern adopted on the following pages.

2.2.1 Stage A: Inception
The RIBA document *Architect's appointment* describes this work stage as follows:

1.1   Discuss the client's requirements including timescale and any financial limits; assess these and give general advice on how to proceed; agree the architect's services.

1.2   Obtain from the client information on ownership and any lessors and lessees of the site, any existing buildings on the site, boundary fences and other enclosures, and any known easements, encroachments, underground services, rights of way, rights of support and other relevant matters.

1.3   Visit the site and carry out an initial appraisal.

1.4   Advise on the need for other consultants' services and on the scope of these services.

1.5   Advise on the need for specialist contractors, subcontractors and suppliers to design and execute part of the works to comply with the architect's requirements.

1.6   Advise on the need for site staff.

1.7   Prepare where required an outline timetable and fee basis for further services for the client's approval.

The list of activities embraced by work stage A is fascinating in its range. To my mind, many of them are misplaced in the timescale and will more usually arise much later in the project's progress. Some may be only touched on at this stage, with more detailed discussion or activity when the form of the project takes clearer shape. But for reasons of form and clarity, they are discussed here.
An architect can probably do more to protect himself at his first meeting with a client than at any future time. We live in a tough economic climate, wherein competition in one form or another may be necessary to survive it all. Anxiety to secure a commission can lead to the discarding of all prudence and discretion, and that first meeting can often lay a pattern of ground-rules that cannot fail to lead to future problems. The recent introduction of fee-competition has probably made matters worse, but only to reinforce the general principle. The temptation to over-sell oneself simply has to be resisted, because the more

expert you claim to be, the more assurances you give about your abilities, resources, and the eventual building, the greater your potential liability. Remember, you carry with you a presumption that you will exercise the skill and care of the average practitioner, and if you claim nothing more than that, then that is the basis on which you will be judged. If you project any specialist expertise, then in that area you will be judged more harshly.

In 30 years I have not come across a practising architect whose opinion of himself and his fellows is such that he does not consider himself considerably better at most things than the 'average competent architect', and most are not shy to say so. Resist the temptation. It so happens that I have acquired a reputation in one particular field, and clients have occasionally referred to me as an 'expert'. I always disabuse them and point out that that epithet is one applied by other people. For myself, I say only that I have had considerable experience and a fair degree of success. Surprisingly, that does not deter them, and they still think of me as an expert. It's a funny world.

If, as is increasingly common, you have a practice brochure, keep it factual and avoid sales-puff. Let the pictures speak for themselves. What is more, keep it up to date. The nature and personnel of a practice change, and yours may well be displaying an image that is no longer correct.

2.2.1.1 *Financial limits and timescale*

While the client's financial limits and timescale may be discussed at the outset of a project, in most cases this will do no more than establish the cash and time parameters within which the feasibility study should be carried out. While a client may know what he is prepared to spend, he seldom has the knowledge to relate it to his requirements, and it should be clearly explained that discussion of budgets must await a later stage. There are real dangers in agreeing to proceed with a project, even through the preliminary stages, on the basis of a firm cost limit. If your preliminary investigations, which can be quite costly, result in the client's aborting the project, you may find yourself whistling for your fees. You may be able to advise your client straight away that he cannot achieve what he wants within his financial or time limits—seldom is the reverse true. Play a potential client like a trout and you may find you have a sting-ray on the end of your line. Claiming fees in these circumstances may often precipitate a counterclaim alleging breach of duty or negligence.

Alternatively, you may be dealing with an 'expert' client who has already carried out his own feasibility study. In these circumstances, financial limits and timescales may be presented as faits accomplis. Whatever else you do at this stage, do not accept the commission with these parameters as a binding condition. You may find on investigation that they are mutually contradictory and that you have taken on an impossible task. It is much better to make your own assessment and present the unwelcome tidings to your client at the outset. As an employed assistant, I was twice presented with impossible time and cost parameters. In each case, when I explained the problem to my employer (one a staid long-established large practice, and the other a booming sole principal), I received the same response: 'Well, you'd better tell them yourself!'. This I duly did and got my employers off a very uncomfortable hook. If I had not been so persistent, both projects would have been unqualified disasters.

2.2.1.2 Site information

It is the responsibility of the client to provide his architect with information about the site. Even if you have handed him a copy of *Architect's appointment*, he is unlikely to volunteer all the information unless you actually ask for it. If he does not yet own the site, he may even not have the information or be able to obtain it. You should always explain in writing the possible effects that site constraints may have on your proposals.

Often, the client will pass the buck back to you to establish the site conditions. If so, you cannot afford to take anything for granted.

2.2.1.3 Site appraisal

Inception usually includes some kind of site appraisal. Even in advance of detailed surveys, there is usually information available from the local authority which may well affect the appraisal. Check all departments: town planning, borough engineer, and highways. Where it may be particularly relevant, check with the statutory supply authorities. Water supplies in particular can be very costly to bring in if the existing mains are inadequate. Check also for rights and easements acquired by adjoining owners. The service of an injunction in the middle of a building contract has been known to test the patience and fray the temper of the mildest and best-disposed client.

2.2.1.4 Advising on the need for consultants

Also in the preliminary stages, the architect has the unenviable task of advising his client on the need for consultants. I deal with the role of consultants below, and here only warn of the general liabilities arising from the advice on the need for consultants and from the recommendation of particular firms.

First let us look at the need for consultants. With major projects and sophisticated clients, the employment of consultants is taken for granted, and you may find that your client will insist on the appointment of consultants for work which you consider to be well within your competence. With smaller projects and lay clients, the reverse is true. The need for consultants is often viewed as no more than a confession of inadequacy by the architect and another burdensome fee for the client to find. The need for consultants is dealt with in the *Architect's appointment*, and insofar as all consultant services are also optional services that may be provided by the architect for additional fees, there ought, on the face of it, to be no difficulty. However, in these days of negotiated fees and fee competition, a client may believe that he will get a better financial deal if his architect can be prevailed upon to provide some or all of the specialist services himself.

A few years ago, in response to a great deal of discontent among clients on the topic of consultants, the RIBA investigated just what an architect could be expected to do for his fee, particularly in the field of structural engineering and services. The findings were, to say the least, inconclusive, although the investigation did provide an intriguing insight into the variety of ways in which the problem was dealt with in practice. In the end, the group concluded that an architect could be expected to be able to do precisely that which he is in his professional judgement considered he was competent to do, which did not really answer the question.

Most commonly, architects rely on the goodwill of a friendly engineer or contractor to fill the gaps in their own knowledge of specialist services. The arrangements are often informal in the extreme, and to all appearances the architect is providing the service unaided. He carries full responsibility for whatever goes out in his name. Often there will be a standing arrangement for an engineer to take on these odd chores on some kind of fee arrangement— generally time-charged—and sometimes the authorship of the service will be declared on drawings, specifications, or calculations. If the architect is providing an all-in service to his client and charging a single fee, then it is to the architect that the client will look for compensation if anything goes wrong. Your insurers will expect to be informed of these arrangements, and if you fail to declare them, you could find yourself without cover when the balloon goes up. If you do inform your insurers, they will probably require evidence of insurance from the specialist. This is so that they may have a chance of recovering their loss through subrogation if there is a claim. Informing your insurers is crucial. It is no use relying on a letter of indemnity from your pet consultant, as you have no way of ensuring that he is insured—or that he will always maintain his insurance.

As the architect is acknowledged as the leader of the building team, it is not inappropriate for him to lay down the manner in which the team should operate. It is good practice to maintain standard procedures for all members of the design team, with special emphasis on the fact that, though appointed by the client, they are the *architect's* consultants. Set out the service you expect from them, the stages at which you expect it, and so on. Hand this document to your client before he appoints the consultants so that you do not find out later that they have been appointed in some more limited role, thereby throwing a greater burden on your own resources.

I have to say that you will not always get away with it, but your position will be immeasurably strengthened if problems arise from the appointment of consultants on terms that conflict with the proper co-ordination of their work. You may not even have to say, 'I told you so!'.

If your client accepts your advice on the need for consultants, he may still want you to appoint them yourself, but this should be avoided if possible. Consortia are dealt with more fully below, but there is really no difficulty in making the appointment 'on behalf of the client' and laying down a direct responsibility. Just make sure that your client knows about it.

Later you may come to the knottiest problem of all—actually recommending consultants. This recommendation is as much professional advice as any other action, and you must bring to the recommendation 'skill and care'. An RIBA Practice Note suggests that you should always provide a list of three names and insist that the client makes his own choice. I have a feeling that all this achieves is a trebling of the burden of skill and care. You have to be in a position to show later that the recommendation was not made negligently. You are quite entitled to rely on established reputations in making a recommendation, and you could hardly be attacked for putting forward a 'household name'. Young practitioners, starting out, like to build relationships with similar young engineers and specialists, where there may be a closer meeting of minds. However praiseworthy and desirable this may be, be as sure as you can that you are not recommending a firm of whose competence to provide the service there may be any doubt.

If things go wrong, you could find yourself as a principal target on the grounds of 'negligent advice'. We all like to give our friends and contemporaries a break, but there are real hazards in being a 'good chap' and they should be guarded against. Indeed, it is probably more important for the young practitioner to stick with established consultants than for the practitioner who has been around for years and may be better able to judge the abilities of a rising firm.

2.2.1.5 Specialist contractors, subcontractors, and suppliers

I suppose that the sooner you can explain to your client the ramifications of the construction industry, the better. If this is his first building project, he won't understand, but it will be off your chest. If you explain fully enough our unique arrangements and the paperwork entailed, he may at least be more reconciled to your fee.

A practice has recently grown amongst clients of seeking a financial bond from subcontractors. It is a regrettable fact that over the past 10 years there have been many bankruptcies and liquidations among subcontractors, and the financial bond, by which a bank or insurance company underwrites the subcontractor's ability to complete, is seen as one line of defence against this contingency. My personal view of bonds is that they are not worth the troubles they present. A real difficulty in timing arises, because the subcontractor will not seek his bond until he is actually nominated, and if there is any doubt about his financial stability, he may not be able to obtain it at all. Either way, one tends to be committed to the subcontractor, with the alternative of submitting the main contractor to delay, and in the final analysis, the client has the protection of the bond only when he doesn't need it.

2.2.1.6 Advice on the need for site staff

You have not even got a building project yet, but now is your chance to disabuse your client of any vision he may have of your own duties of inspection—not that this will avail you greatly if there is an eventual building failure shown to be due to defective workmanship. It is as well to advise the client at this stage that the need for site staff may not become apparent until much later in the process. Particularly, the need may not become apparent until you are considering the acceptance of tenders, or even later, when you have evidence of defective performance by the builder on site. Warn the client at this stage, and you may have much less trouble if and when the need actually arises. Site staff can add appreciably to the all-up cost of a project, but if there is no provision for it, you may find yourself carrying out far more site inspections than were ever allowed for within your fee.

2.2.1.7 Timetable

More haste—less heed. There cannot be an architect practising who has not, on occasions, had to work to a programme that he knows to be shorter than he requires to perform adequately. Many of the cases being settled today have their roots in the overheated building booms of the early 1960s and early 1970s. Few clients understand the full process of building procurement, and some may point to project times achieved in other countries when attempting to lay down completion dates for their projects. Certainly, the organisation and methods most usually employed in England seem designed to extend construction programmes to near eternity. There are signs that things are changing, but in the conventional process there is an order of events that cannot be avoided, and abiding by the procedures does take time. So do try to get your programmes right from the start. Don't forget that inevitably you will be waiting on input from specialists, manufacturers, and suppliers. Don't forget that your quantity surveyor, working to SMM6, will require from you all the details that a few years ago would not have been required until the builder was on site—not to mention some that the builder should not need at all.

And don't forget to instruct your client on his responsibility for providing information and approvals promptly.

A realistic programme, agreed with your client at the outset, is probably your best defence against future errors.

2.2.1.8 Fee basis for further service

It is difficult to advise on how to deal with fees at an 'inception' meeting. Although stages A and B are on a time-charge basis, the client will generally want to know what his commitment will be, both if the project aborts and if it proceeds. What's sauce for the goose . . . Just as the client may wish to know his commitment, so it is imperative that the architect should know what he is undertaking. The golden rule is not to commit yourself until you know just what it is you are in for. And with so much depending on the client himself, you may not know that until the job is complete. It is, however, my firm belief that much of the criticism thrown at architects derives from their too-hasty agreements on fixed fees for unknown and elastic quantities of work. Inadequate fees lead almost inevitably to corner-cutting, with the resultant risk. With the loss of the architect's mandatory fee scale, you can no longer rely on the 'swings and roundabouts', because you will probably have to accept lower fees for those large, simple jobs that used to pay for all the rest.

The following information may not be absolutely typical, but it does show what I mean. An analysis of fees earned on 20 jobs in my own office disclosed the information that the earning capacity of jobs varied by a factor of seven! At the bottom of the scale, each hour of technical time produced £6.60 of fees, and at the top each similar hour earned £44.50. These jobs were all charged on the basis of the old 'purple book'—more or less. The full table is given on p 71. While the earning rate shows an overall correlation to job size, there are a number of projects where this does not apply. Some years ago, I was called in by a property developer when a small development had gone sour. The job, the refurbishment and conversion of a small commercial property, had been halted by a Dangerous Structures Notice, the builder had disappeared, and the client, understandably, had lost confidence in his architect. Investigation disclosed the most appalling catalogue of incompetence, recklessness, and neglect that I have ever come across, which in the report I prepared were summarised as follows:

1 Recommending Builder A to carry out the contract works at a figure the architect had already assessed as being incapable of achievement

2 Recommending the acceptance of an unreasonably low price without warning his client of the possible consequences

3 Procuring his client to become party to an unsuitable form of contract which offered him no protection other than in damages for breach and placed him in financial jeopardy from the outset

4 Using the RIBA minor works form of contract despite the warning on the form that it was unsuitable

5 Not procuring a priced specification and schedule of rates

6 Failing to provide adequate drawings and instructions for the proper execution of the works

7 Writing into a contract a requirement the effect of which was to bind the contractor to illegal acts in respect of VAT

8 Relying on the builder's verbal assurances that he had incurred certain expenditure without requiring the submission of any kind of written proof, thereby grossly over-certifying

9 Permitting or procuring Mr B to take over the works in the name of Builder A

10 Continuing to write and sign certificates for the benefit of Builder A while payment was actually being made direct to third parties

11 Failing to advise the client of his rights against Builder A, or of the procedure which should have been followed in order to safeguard those rights when Builder A defected

12 Taking upon himself responsibility for structural design for which he was clearly not qualified

13 Permitting the builder to execute works which were either not in accordance with the specification or not good building practice

14   Failing to require the builder to remedy unsatisfactory, defective, and dangerous work

15   Instructing the builder to remove the major part of the basement front wall without either giving him clear instructions on how to do it or assuring himself that the builder was competent to do it

16   Failing to deal properly with party wall matters

There was, in fact, a seventeenth negligent act, because the architect had failed to insure himself adequately!

The background to this sorry saga was one which I suspect is all too common. The client, who should have known better, had persuaded the architect to accept a fee basis which was inadequate from the outset, and where the fees anyway were hostage if the job failed to proceed. When the job tenders came in above the client's budget (and the architect's initial estimate), the project was in danger of aborting, and the architect, rightly or wrongly, was probably in fear for his fees. So he found a builder who was prepared to carry out the work for a figure that was within the budget. The builder was a man of straw, of doubtful ability, and required payment in advance.

When the builder predictably disappeared, leaving a shambles of a half–demolished building behind him, the architect persuaded the foreman to continue on a cash basis, after which things went, if conceivable, from bad to worse. The client's loss approached £100,000, and the architect's cover was a mere £25,000. In the end, the client took the insurance money, plus a token payment from the architect, and swallowed his £60,000 losses.

Subsequently, I have thought a lot about this case. Almost every idiotic, reckless, and, I suspect, fraudulent action taken by the luckless architect can be ascribed, at least in part, to the unsatisfactory financial basis of the whole transaction. A one-man firm just cannot afford to take on work that is labour-intensive unless the fee is adequate to support him. If he allows his fees, on which he depends just to live, to be held hostage in respect of events over which he has little or no control, then calamity will surely follow. At no time was he guilty of bad faith towards his client. All he was trying to do was to keep the job going with inadequate resources. That pressing need seems to have over-ruled all his professional judgements and discretion—truly a case of money being the root of all evil.

The ironic sequel, if you have not already guessed, is that my own practice sustained an extremely heavy loss on the rescue operation, but because the project was a small one, it was supported by other, larger jobs in the office. In subsequent work for the same client, who is now an older and wiser man, we get the financial arrangements right from the outset.

Never over-sell yourself

Checklist: Inception

1   Never over-sell yourself.

2   Do not accept budgets or timescales without making your own assessment.

3   Make your own site investigations and take nothing for granted.

4   Try to ensure that the client appoints consultants direct—*for a service that accords with your needs*.

5   Reserve your right to request site staff (or additional site staff) if the need becomes apparent.

6   Insist on an adequate timescale.

7   Get the fee basis right at the outset.

2.2.2 Collateral agreements
Elsewhere in this book I deal with the tortious duty that an architect owes to third parties. Onerous as you may consider that duty to be, there are many third parties around who, from either lack of understanding of the law or excessive prudence, seek to improve their protection by way of collateral agreements.
When an architect is commissioned by a client, his contract is direct and personal between himself and an individual or a firm. More often than not, his client is no more than an intermediary in the building procurement process. On the one side there may be a bank, institution, or funding organisation that will be providing the finance for the development, and on the other there may be an eventual owner, or tenant, or user, for whose benefit the building is actually being erected. The bank, funding organisation, eventual owner, or user has a very real interest in the proceedings, and it is to protect those interests that the collateral agreement has been devised.

2.2.2.1 The funding organisation
We will first consider the position of the funding organisation. Developers commonly have two separate sources of finance—short-term or bridging, and long-term or eventual sale. The short-term or bridging loan is commonly secured by way of a mortgage on the property, and there is often an agreement with a second institution to purchase the completed development at an agreed figure once it is fully let. Even if the building is being erected for the client's own occupation, similar arrangements may apply, with a sale and leaseback arrangement agreed in advance in respect of the completed building.

Should something go wrong in the course of the development, and that will normally be the failure or financial embarrassment of the client, the funding organisation providing the bridging finance will become the owner of the property. If the reason is the financial failure of your client, then your professional appointment is at an end. In all probability, because (unlike a funding organisation) the architect seldom takes reasonable steps to secure his fees, he may be owed a considerable sum of money. At the same time, the fund will have come into possession of a part-completed development, with a building contract that may have been breached by the failure of the employer. The funding organisation may well have a collateral agreement with the builder to accept an assignment of his contract to the fund so that the development can continue with the least possible disruption.

In a case like this, the fund has two interests in relation to the architect that it will seek to safeguard by agreement. First, that the architect recognises his general duty to the fund, who may become the owner and who is therefore relying on the skill and care of the architect in the performance of his professional duties. Second, the fund will want to ensure that the architect will continue to act. While the collateral agreements I have seen may be exceptions, the terms are always outrageously in favour of the fund and to the detriment of the architect. My advice, for what it is worth, is to refuse to enter into collateral agreements if you possibly can.

The *Architect's appointment* recognises the personal nature of the contract between the architect and his client. One of the most important clauses in the *Conditions of engagement* is the right of either party to terminate the appointment on giving reasonable notice. The collateral agreement almost certainly overrides that clause and binds you to the fund to see the commission through to completion. Usually, the fund will undertake to pay the architect's fees *from the time they accept the ownership of the site*. Usually, the fund rejects specifically any liability for outstanding fees.

In my own practice, it has always been a cardinal rule that we will not accept or agree to accept any commission from an unknown client. We want to know who we are working for, and we are not happy to work for any client who is prepared to employ an unknown architect, sight unseen. We have always taken the view that, if for any reason the client disposes of his site, we will be prepared to meet the new owner to discuss a possible reappointment. We accept his right to appoint a new architect and insist on our own right not to work for him if for any reason we do not think that the conditions are suitable or the relationship will be an amicable one. It has been my personal experience that banks and funds appreciate this standpoint and are prepared to accept it.

There are a number of points that it is as well to bear in mind. If you already have a formal appointment from your client, nobody can actually require you to enter into a collateral agreement. True, in extreme cases, the development may founder or the client may decide that he has to go to a more malleable architect, but if he is handled properly this is unlikely to happen. If, on the other hand, you are asked *as a condition of your appointment* to enter into a collateral agreement, then you may feel that you have little or no option. In cases like this, insist on meeting representatives of the fund—in particular, those representatives to whom you will be looking for your instructions if, at the worst, your client does default. If you are not happy with the set-up, then you will be foolish to agree.

Look at the terms of the agreement. If necessary, get them checked over by your solicitor and your insurers to ascertain that they do not place on you any greater burden than you are already subjected to by the law of tort. Positively insist that the terms of your appointment by the fund will be no different from the terms of appointment that you have enjoyed with your original client. Insist particularly that the whole agreement is conditional upon the fund's accepting responsibility for any fees which may be outstanding to you at the time of your client's default. Do not agree to release copyright to the new owners unless you have been properly paid for the work. These are all quite reasonable requirements, and while they may not be volunteered in the first draft of a collateral agreement, if the fund will not agree to them, then it is not the sort of organisation for whom any prudent architect would wish to act.

2.2.2.2 The eventual user

The position with the eventual owners, users, or occupiers is a little different, but the principle is the same. It does not take a formal agreement for the architect to acknowledge the interest of the eventual owner. In tort, that interest cannot be greater than the duty that the architect owes his client, but collateral agreements with eventual occupants very often imply a warranty of 'fitness for purpose'. Particularly on inspection, they may impose greater duties than one owes one's client under the architect's appointment. Badly drawn collateral agreements can often create major conflicts between your duty to your client and the duty to the third party.

The view I take on collateral agreements is fairly simple. For the architect they are full of pitfalls, and for the third parties they are probably not worth the paper they are written on. Resist them if you can, but if you see no alternative to agreeing to them, remember that they are legal and binding contracts and take advice from your lawyers and insurers on the precise wording.

Checklist: Collateral agreements

1   Avoid collateral agreements if possible.

2   If you cannot avoid them, have them vetted by a lawyer.

3   Use them to safeguard your fees.

2.2.3 Stage B: Feasibility and brief
The *Architect's appointment* describes this work stage as follows.

1.8   Carry out such studies as may be necessary to determine the feasibility of the client's requirements; review with the client alternative design and construction approaches and cost implications; advise on the need to obtain planning permissions, approvals under building acts or regulations, and other similar statutory requirements.

The on-running effect of this preliminary stage of a project cannot be over-emphasised, and the care with which this part of the service is carried out is crucial.

2.2.3.1 Feasibility studies

Feasibility covers a multitude of operations, from major social, industrial, or economic studies, to a simple assessment of the possibilities of converting a garage into a living room. The inadequacy of a feasibility study will usually come to light before any physical building takes place, and in such cases the client's losses may be limited to the fees he has incurred. But he may have acquired an unsuitable site that he will be able to sell only at a loss, and have incurred other costs and expenses which he will be unable to recover.

I see much advice published nowadays about the need for architects to develop greater commercial awareness. They are encouraged to study the factors used in commerce and the development industry for assessing viability. Many architects pride themselves on their ability to present commercial viability studies, which they use to promote schemes of one kind or another.

Certainly, if you are involved in commercial development, you will need to know how your client carries out his viability study and how viability is affected by changes in the criteria which fall within the responsibility of the architect. But some factors are outside the general competence or expertise of the architect, and it is here that a major risk arises. When architects present total viability studies on the basis of which a client purchases a site at the wrong price, the architect could well be held liable for the loss. By and large, developers are a philosophical breed and tend to lick their wounds, but it is better not to rely on this: often they are not masters of their own fate, and the fund which is standing behind them may not be so forgiving. Anyway, you will probably have lost a client.

2.2.3.2 Collecting the brief

Collecting the brief is another task to be performed with both care and judgement. Detailed briefing will follow later, and probably in a well structured fashion, but clients' initial briefs tend to be a mixture of long-term requirement, transmitted experience, and preconceived solutions. Hold everything! I am probably telling most of my readers nothing they do not already know when I say that many clients are almost unbelievably ignorant, either of their own requirements and the alternative solutions available to them, or of the way in which their previous experience may be quite inapplicable in changed circumstances.

So always question your client's brief. Sort out just what is a true requirement, and what is no more than a casual reference to a presumed solution. The architect's perception at briefing stage may well be the most valuable talent he can provide to his client. At best, failure to question the brief may simply result in a not very good solution to the client's real problem; at worst, it can involve you in the risk of a claim.

A typical and trivial incident illustrates the point. Newly in practice, I took my client's brief on a shopfitting job, for a trader with a substantial chain of camera shops long since absorbed into a much larger company. Included in the brief was a clear instruction for the display shelves to be 14in. from the window glass. All went well until the day before the opening, when I received a phone call from an extremely irate client.

'We can't dress the windows—the shelves are too close to the glass!'

'But they are 14in. clear.'

'Well, it's not enough.'

'But that's what you asked for.'

'I don't care about that—YOU'RE THE ARCHITECT!'

Of course, he was quite right, and I had learned a very valuable lesson.

2.2.3.3 The need to obtain planning permission

It is necessary to spell out to a client as early as possible the implications of his need to obtain planning permission. But first establish whether the need exists. A great deal of building work does not actually require planning permission, either because it does not constitute development or because it has 'deemed consent'. Your client will not thank you for obtaining a permission he did not require in the first place, delaying his project for months in the process.

With the growth of refurbishment, there are many grey areas. One such is the option to 'materially alter the external appearance of a building' or leave it as it is. With the delays inherent in the planning system, gratuitously subjecting your client's project to control for the satisfaction of your own ego could be held to be a very damaging breach of duty.

I could, but probably won't, write a book on the defects in our planning law. The introduction of fees for planning applications I considered to be an iniquity unparalleled elsewhere in British law. Together with Premium Bonds, it is the only state-sponsored lottery: unlike any other approval in the construction industry, obtaining permission is not dependent on complying with stated criteria, however ill-expressed and confusing they may be. The granting or refusal of planning permission rests with a lay committee where members may exercise their own views, prejudices, and preferences, or be influenced by vociferous minorities, political infighting, or an approaching election. True, there is a right of appeal, but that involves more delay and expense.

So explain very carefully to your client that it is not within your power to *obtain* planning permission—only to apply for it. Explain also that the design may have to be quite fully developed before the planning authority will even consider it. Finally, explain that consulting with the authority's officers and amending proposals to meet their suggestions is no guarantee that the committee will accept their officer's recommendations.

Checklist: Stage B

---

1 Commercial feasibility studies require specialist expertise.

---

2 Always question your client's brief.

---

3 Never undertake to *obtain* planning permission.

2.2.4 Stages C and D: Preliminary design
The *Architect's appointment* describes these work stages as follows:

1.9 With other consultants where appointed, analyse the client's requirements; prepare outline proposals and an approximation of the construction cost for the client's preliminary approval.

1.10 With other consultants where appointed, develop a scheme design from
the outline proposals; prepare a cost estimate; where applicable give an
indication of possible start and completion dates for the building contract. The scheme design will illustrate the size and character of the
project in sufficient detail to enable the client to agree the spatial arrangements, materials, and appearance.

Having disposed of the preliminaries, hopefully without having set a long fuse
on some inherent time-bomb, an architect embarks on the main objective of
his appointment—a design for the project. You might think that in this area the
architect is at greatest risk, but you would be quite wrong. Although he may
make decisions at this stage which can lead to later problems, it is extremely
rare for an architect to be sued in respect of inherent defects in his general
design. More particularly, architects are never sued in respect of the appearance of the design.

2.2.4.1. The importance of a correct budget
Probably the most important factor at the design stage is to ensure that the
design is capable of being achieved within the client's budget—or that you
establish a budget which is adequate to accommodate the design. Probably,
more problems can be traced back to inadequate budgets than any other single
cause. It is likely that financial considerations figure too prominently in the
design of buildings, especially first cost.
The achievement of the design within budget has other implications for architects. There are countless cases of clients aborting schemes which are outside
budget—and then refusing to pay their architect's fees. Pressing for fees in these
circumstances has an unfortunate habit of boomeranging as a complaint about
defective service, which may grow into a full-scale lawsuit.

2.2.4.2 The role of the quantity surveyor
It has been said that a quantity surveyor is a man who knows the price of every-

thing and the value of nothing. Certainly the training and the principal activities of the quantity surveyor are directed to the detailed analysis of the physical components of a building for the purpose of then synthesising a total cost. In this principal activity the quantity surveyor has no need to exercise judgement or imagination; the process is formalised and mechanical, relying heavily on published data and personal experience. Accordingly, quantity surveyors are deeply suspicious of anything that departs from well trodden paths, or relies for an appreciation of its value on the application of imagination and judgement, the very qualities that are central to the role of the architect. In the words of the New York cop in an ancient TV series, 'Give me the facts ma'am, I just want the facts'.

In the creation of a building design, facts are at a premium and judgement is all-important. Too often the judgement is marred by financial advice prejudiced by the quantity surveyor's suspicion of the unknown and his need at all costs to preserve his credibility with the client.

I have dim and fading recollections of an architect/quantity surveyor relationship quite unlike today's. The quantity surveyor, in addition to his role of measurer and recorder of the physical components of a building, was the architect's adviser, whose role was to assist the architect in establishing budgets and developing the design. Today, increasingly, he is the client's man, and all this talk about the design team is more often than not a falsification of the true relationship. The quantity surveyor's task commonly is to dragoon the architect into the straightjacket of costing preconceptions dictated by SMM5, SMM6, or whatever costings convention is currently the rage. Clients understand, or like to think they understand, money talk. The sooner architects re-colonise that area of the design process, the better. There is little the quantity surveyor does that cannot be better done by a micro-computer, and the micro doesn't charge fees!

2.2.4.3 *Know your building law*

Within the preliminary design process, the architect needs to give adequate consideration to the mountain of legislation applicable to buildings: in the area of legislation the architect is expected to *know*! Building legislation develops in cycles, commencing with unarguable basic requirements and becoming more tortuous, complex, and contradictory as it receives the impact of committees of investigation, working parties, codes of practice, standards, Agrément certificates, ministry circulars, edicts, and statutory orders. Know your building law! Easier said than done, perhaps, but contravening any of the legislation will lead you into trouble with no way out.

One tiny piece of relief was granted by the Court of Appeal a few years ago in the case of *British Land Holdings Ltd* v *Robert J Wood & Partners*. Here the architect was so trusting as to accept the view of the planning officer at Brighton that he had no need to include the area of basement carparking in his calculations for an office development permit. After the building was complete, the planning authority had second thoughts and the original consent was held to be invalid. In possession of a building that had no planning permission, the owners, British Land, sued the architects for their loss, and in the lower court

QS replaced by micro-computer

they won, the learned judge holding that the architect should have known the rules about ODPs. I confess that I agreed with the judge, albeit with some reservations, because the client was an experienced developer and could hardly have failed to know just what was going on. In the event, the appeal court found for the architect, holding that he was entitled to rely on the local planning authority for a ruling on the planning law. This was an interesting case, with far-reaching implications. As one who has often criticised officials for not knowing or understanding the law they have to administer, I had always assumed that one could *not* rely on the advice of officers. Certainly I never did, and despite the ruling of the appeal court, I will continue to use my own understanding and judgement in interpreting building legislation.

2.2.4.4 Site information
Preliminary design is the stage when the architect needs to know all about the site he is working on. Whatever his appointment may say about the client's responsibility for providing the information, the architect has an obligation to request the information. Too often, designs are formulated without good site information, with dire results in later stages of the design or construction process.

2.2.4.5 Traditional or innovative design
Preliminary design is the time when architects decide upon the type of construction they intend to employ. What may have been no more than a thought tucked away at the back of the mind, may now be brought out for translation into fact. This is when an architect will decide whether to employ traditional methods or some innovation in material, product, or technique. Architects are often criticised for innovation, particularly when things go wrong—but without innovation there would be no progress and we would still be building in wattle and daub. There is nothing wrong with innovation, but it does impose additional burdens of care on the architect. It is not to be undertaken lightly, and the necessary research must be undertaken with care. It is, anyway, a fact that a majority of the defects in buildings arise from 'traditional' construction inadequately detailed or executed. I use the quotation marks deliberately because there are at least grounds for doubting whether there is anything that can truly be called 'traditional' construction today. Certainly a component as basic as a brick wall bears little resemblance to the brick walls I learned in Mitchell or Mackay. Advancing technology changes everything, from the composition of the bricks and mortar to the method of assembly.
Preliminary design is also when satisfaction of the brief is achieved—or not. Sometimes the brief may be in part only implied. I have heard of one case where a developer client sued his architect because he produced a design that was not financially viable. This was not a case of failing to meet a budget, but of failure to produce a design providing sufficient lettable space. As the firm concerned was commissioned because of its experience in development work, one can at least understand why the client was aggrieved. I don't know the facts of the case or the outcome, but I can understand how the problems might have arisen. The project was a comparatively small one in a large firm. Often such

Innovation means extra risk

projects are delegated to young architects who do not themselves have the experience for which the firm is noted. This raises the whole question of delegation of responsibility within firms. Clearly, delegation is both necessary and desirable, but with it goes a responsibility for supervision. Neglect it at your peril.

Preliminary design is quite likely to throw up discrepancies and contradictions in the brief. These simply have to be resolved with the client. The architect cannot take upon himself the onus of allocating priority to the various elements of a client's brief. When, after discussion, the priorities have been decided, do not fail to record it. Your records will serve you better than your memory a few years hence.

2.2.4.6 Presentation of proposals

Last, but by no means least, prepare for the client proper reports on your outline and scheme designs. The simple act of preparing a structured report is a wonderful discipline and will not only remind you of the constraints and balances on which your proposals are based: it may even remind you in time of factors you may have overlooked. Either way, it will form a permanent record of just how your proposals were developed. Many architects present schemes to clients 'across the table' or with a simple covering letter. In subsequent discussions, deprived of the benefit of a formal report, they may agree to admendments with dire effects later in the day. A report will keep you on course during these discussions.

The reports will be a record of the skill and care brought to the design process and will serve you in good stead if, much later, the client's priorities having changed, you are charged with having overlooked some now-crucial requirements, which at the time of the design process had a much lower priority.

Checklist: Stages C and D

1 Watch the budget.

2 Know your building law—all of it.

3 Check your site information.

4 Innovation implies a special duty of care.

5 Clear with your client all departures from the brief.

6 Delegation imposes a duty of supervision.

7 Submit full written reports with your proposals.

2.2.5 Stages E, F, and G: Detail design, production information, and bills of quantities
I have lumped together work stages E, F, and G because on most projects they
are inextricably intertwined. The official counsel of perfection not to commence any work stage before completion of the previous one was ever
honoured in the breach, and the conditions set out in the *Architect's appointment*
simply state that no work stage should be commenced without the approval of
the client. What else does the *Architect's appointment* have to say about these work
stages?

1.13   With other consultants where appointed, develop the scheme design;
obtain the client's approval of the type of construction, quality of
materials and standard of workmanship; co-ordinate any design work
done by consultants, specialist contractors, subcontractors and suppliers;
obtain quotations and other information in connection with specialist
work.

1.14   With other consultants where appointed, carry out cost checks as necessary; advise the client of the consequences of any subsequent changes on
the cost and programme.

1.15   Make and negotiate where required applications for approvals under
building acts, regulations or other statutory requirements. With other
consultants where appointed, prepare production information including
drawings, schedules and specification of materials and workmanship;
provide information for bills of quantities, if any, to be prepared: all
information complete in sufficient detail to enable a contractor to prepare
a tender.

The scope for committing what might be adjudged an omission or act of
negligence during these stages is almost boundless, and it is difficult to prescribe
any sure-fire procedures for staying safe. Practices vary enormously in size,
organisation, design philosophy, and available skills, while projects vary
similarly in size and complexity over an almost infinite range.
There are, however, some golden rules that apply right across the board.

2.2.5.1 Honest self-appraisal
Know thyself! The best judge of an architect's capabilities, or of those of a
practice, is the architect himself. An honest appraisal of one's skills, knowledge,
and resources, and a determination to work within them, is not only a professional obligation under the Code of Conduct, it is a very good starting point for
staying clear of trouble. We cannot all be Norman Fosters, and if hi-tech is not
your forte, then stick with neo-vernacular, traditional, modern, or whatever else
you are good at.

2.2.5.2 Keep up to date
Building technology is developing continually, and in years to come your
actions will be judged by 'the state of the art' at the time you committed them.

Keeping up to date is no easy task—there's a lot of books, journals, digests, practice notes, acts and statutory instruments, and codes of practice. There is no short cut, and keeping up to date is a continuing process. Every practising professional should consciously work at the process, and in his own sphere of work should ensure that all the latest promulgated advice is readily available to him. The problem is particularly acute for the lone practitioner, who tends to work in a less-than-splendid isolation. A simple piece of advice: join your local branch of the RIBA—and go to the meetings! Go not necessarily for what is on the agenda, but for simple contact with other architects. It is in the informal conversations before and after the business of the meeting that you learn what is new.

Delegation implies supervision. At the end of the day, it is the principal who accepts responsibility for everything done in his name. You may think that you know the skills and abilities of your staff, but it implies no lack of trust for you to satisfy yourself that the product is correct. The professional press is regrettably bespattered with advertisements for 'architect, minimum three years experience, able to run projects with minimum supervision'. The principal asset of your practice may be your own twenty years experience—use it!

Most title blocks on architects' drawings carry space for names 'drawn by' and 'checked by'. If I had 10p for every blank 'checked by' block, I could retire to my tropical paradise tomorrow!

2.2.5.3 Innovation equals extra risk

While it is a fact that a very high proportion of building claims arises from defective detailing of quite common forms of construction, the adoption of new materials, components, or methods of construction presents a real enhancement of risk. Not only is it necessary to have special care in deciding the suitability of the innovation and its detailing, there is the added complication that the builder will be looking to you to make sure he gets it right on site.

There are three kinds of innovation: those devised by the architect himself, those marketed to him by suppliers of materials or components, and those which might be publicized in the professional press. For your own re-invented wheel, you have only yourself to blame. For the rest, to what extent can you safely rely on the published information or the representations of the supplier? Not very far! Buildings are complex artefacts, wherein the interplay of the various components and materials comes to be understood only after a fairly long period in use. New materials and components tend to be developed and tested in a technological vacuum. The physical context in which a component or material will be used may significantly affect its performance, and the component or material itself may affect the performance or efficacy of an adjacent material or component.

If you are contemplating using a new material or component, make your own independent enquiries about it. It is many years since the material and component suppliers gave up employing salesmen. Today they are all 'technical representatives', or 'technical sales consultants', or some other similarly misleading title. Some of the older ones are those you would remember from the time when they were salesmen, and it is a fact that the technical abilities and knowledge of the battalions who besiege your office with their brochures and samples leaves, in the main, something to be desired. However, if they profess to expertise, you, in law, are entitled to rely on it. If you present these specialists with a problem (and I do mean the whole problem) and they provide you with a solution, then if something goes wrong, you may have an available third party to bear part or all of the liability. But I do emphasise that you have to show them the whole of the problem. The full context in which a material or component is to be used is extremely important. A dpc material that is quite satisfactory used horizontally in a solid wall may perform entirely differently when spanning a cavity or formed into a stepped apron.

It should be borne in mind that building materials and components increasingly are developed, designed, and manufactured abroad. What may be suitable and sufficient in Scandinavia, Germany, or Spain may not necessarily be suitable and sufficient in the United Kingdom's unique climatic and construction environment.

If you are innovating, you just cannot be too careful.

2.2.5.4 *The control of consultants*

Insist on adequate information from your consultants. I have referred elsewhere to the difficulties that arise from the way in which consultants work, a process which is not synchronised with the architectural detailing process at all. Inadequate information from consultants may be the cause of problems which will not come to light until construction is in progress. Much of the consultant's work is controlled under the Building Regulations and other legislation. Insist that your consultants obtain all the necessary consents and approvals for their own work at a stage early enough for it to be incorporated in details without the need for later revisions.

2.2.5.5 *Allow sufficient time for the process*

Over the past few years, the whole process of preparing production information has had to be dramatically re-programmed, because of a change in two external circumstances. Since the notorious *Anns* v *Merton* decision, building control officers have become extremely mindful of their own liability in law, and either out of a genuine fear for their own safety or because of the opportunity the case gave them to increase their authority and power, they now commonly insist on being provided with vast quantities of detailed and technical information which was previously taken for granted. Similarly, the adoption of SMM6 by quantity surveyors has created the need for providing highly detailed drawings many months before they are actually required for the building process. Indeed, because they are working in the isolation of their offices, quantity surveyors today commonly ask for more detailed and explicit drawings than would actually be required by the builder working on site. All of this means that contract lead–in times are being inordinately extended, a circumstance not understood by clients, who continue to exert pressure on their architects and professional team generally to get the contractor on site. For the architect, there is no real answer to this dilemma, although the client has available to him the alternatives of package deal, design/build, or fast-track arrangements, which go

some way to answering the problem. This is a topic to which the profession
and the RIBA must urgently apply themselves if architecture as it has
previously been practised is not to be driven into a cul-de-sac, with a gaping
abyss at the far end.

2.2.5.6 The bill of quantities

I do not suppose there is a single reader of this book who would be so naive as to
ask why I should devote a section to what is quite clearly the product of another
profession. The bill of quantities has assumed an importance in the building
process quite disproportionate to its original intent. Essentially, the bill of
quantities and the standard method by which it is prepared arose because of the
need to provide standard information on which builders could tender for a job,
knowing that each of his competitors had precisely the same clear and un-
ambiguous information on which to carry out his pricing operation. Further, it
provides a basis for the pricing of variations in the work as the contract proceeds. Under the standard form of contract, the following are contract documents: the articles of agreement, the contract conditions, the contract drawings,
and the bill of quantities.

What goes into the bill of quantities is what the builder contracts to build for the
sum he has tendered. The bill of quantities consists of three separate parts:
preliminaries, preambles, and the measured work. Errors and omissions
excepted, the architect is responsible for everything that goes into the first two
sections—the quantity surveyor merely writes it. In no small part, the
dominance that the quantity surveyor has achieved in the building process is a
direct result of the way in which architects have resigned their responsibilities in
practice for the bill of quantities and its contents. It is because the architect is
responsible for so much of what goes into the bill of quantities that quantity
surveyors themselves seldom, if ever, figure in liability suits. In theory anyway, they are merely doing what they are told. So make sure you tell them.
Every quantity surveyor approaches his task armed with three weapons: the
Standard Method of Measurement (5 or 6 with 7 to come), his standard
preliminaries and preambles, and his blank query sheets.
The rationale behind a standard method of measurement is unarguable. It
removes any ambiguity from the descriptions of work and lays down what is
included or allowed for, or excluded, in any particular description, so enabling a
builder to price accurately the particular item. There is little doubt that the
need for precision and unambiguity has been grossly over-estimated, making
the bill of quantities an extremely voluminous document, wherein 30 per cent or
40 per cent of the work is covered in about 5 per cent of the items and 80 per
cent of the value certainly in no more than 20 per cent. This has been
recognised, even by the quantity surveyors, and the proposed SMM7 does go
some way to correcting the balance. It also goes some considerable way to
enabling the architect to write his own bills of quantities, so maybe the tide is
beginning to turn.

2.2.5.7 The preliminary clauses (contract conditions)

It is in the standard preliminary clauses that the architect needs to be on his guard, for it is here that decisions have to be made on the form of contract to be used, any amendments which shall be made to the standard form, and the items or amounts or times to be included in the appendix. These are all matters which the architect should discuss and agree with his client. It is the client who becomes a party to the contract and if, on your advice (or failure to advise), the client is committed to something which was not his intention or under-standing, then you could be in trouble. Periodically it will be claimed by opponents of various standard forms that the architect who advises his client to sign any particular form could be in danger of being sued in negligence for that simple fact alone. Standard forms being what they are, they will never please everybody. In 1973, a special general meeting was held at the RIBA on the proposition that the institute should withdraw from the Joint Contracts Tribunal, and Peter Lord Smith, an ardent campaigner on contracts, made that very point. Similar allegations have been made about JCT '80, with the advice to stick to JCT '63. And with the appearance of a further contract produced by the Association of Consultant Architects, at least one widely published com-mentator has made exactly the same point about that contract.

Provided you have explained to your client the implications of the contract, there is no danger whatsoever in recommending the use of one of the standard published forms. None of the standard forms is so unfairly balanced as to be 'void for inequity', and while one party or the other may consider that some of the terms are unfairly weighted in favour of the other party, the balance of responsibility will also be reflected in the contract sum where there has been competitive tendering. In other words, you get what you pay for, and it is only important that the parties should actually understand the terms.

If you are adopting one of the standard forms—and they are proliferating like rabbits at the present time—simply ensure that you use a form which is appropriate to the job in hand, and that the procedures can be followed within the contract programme. Most problems with contracts arise from the simple cause that the architect cannot go through the administrative procedures, particularly in relation to subcontractors, within the time allowed. Failure to comply with the contract conditions in this way puts the client in breach of con-tract, and the architect could well find himself liable for extra costs which arise in that way. The matters which need to be discussed and agreed with the client primarily are those concerned with possession of the site, contract period, extensions of time, liquidated and ascertained damages, subcontractors, possession and insurance.

2.2.5.8 Possession of the site

You might think this almost superfluous, but surprisingly few sites are actually vacant and in the possession of the client at the time you are preparing the con-tract. The client must be advised when the site has to be available and the con-sequences to him if he fails to arrange it. If the project is an extension of existing premises, then you must discuss with your client just what space and access are going to be available in the building and what access (even occasional access) the client may need through the builder's site in order to continue run-ning his business or other operation. The contractor is entitled to clear and uninterrupted possession of his site and the access to it, subject only to whatever constraints are written into the contract in that respect. Failure to provide that possession and access could amount to a fundamental breach of the contract, and it could result in an exceptionally heavy claim or in the contractor walking off the job altogether.

2.2.5.9 Contract period
Almost inevitably, your client will ask for a contract period which is shorter than a builder will voluntarily offer. There is no such thing as a 'correct' contract period for any particular project, and there is a fairly wide range of time covering what might be termed an 'economic period'. Lesser or greater periods may have their financial implications, and your advice on this should be clear and unequivocal.

2.2.5.10 Extension of time
Not even the Wizard of Oz can guarantee that a building project commenced on time will finish on the due date. Whatever one may feel about the fairness of Clause 20 (25) in JCT '80 or Clause 23 in JCT '63, these clauses merely set out the realities of building operations. In a sense, whether or not there are provisions for extending the contract period is immaterial. Delays will occur, and if they are serious enough, there may simply be no physical method whereby the time lost can be regained. It is important to explain this to your client so that he does not commit himself irrevocably to some course of action which depends precisely upon the contract completion date. If time is the essence of the contract, then it is necessary to establish this and to take whatever steps are necessary in amending the contract to ensure so far as possible that the client's interest is not prejudiced. Certain of the 'grounds' are commonly deleted from the contract, notably those concerning the availability of labour and materials and delays by subcontractors. These are matters which can be within the control of the builder, but it might cost extra money to place them there. Similarly, the clauses relating to exceptionally inclement weather and to strikes and lockouts may be deleted, but possibly at even more considerable cost. (I have never understood why a lockout—a voluntary action totally within the control of the contractor—was ever made a ground for extension of time, but that is by the way.)
What you cannot write out of the contract are those grounds for extension of time which are wholly and solely within the control of the client or his direct agents (and that includes yourself). Extra works, architect's instructions, or delay in the issue of instructions or details are clearly matters for which the builder cannot carry responsibility, and the client should be brought to an understanding of this. Delay in the issue of instructions, if it has not been brought about by the client's delay in making a decision, is something which is squarely on the architect's shoulders.
Even delays by consultants may give rise to liability by the architect if he has failed to lay down and agree a firm programme for the consultants' work. The co-ordination and integration of the work of consultants is part of the architect's basic service.

2.2.5.11 Defects liability period

There is widespread misunderstanding of the meaning, effect, and import of the defects liability period written into most building contracts. Essentially, the DLP is for the protection of the builder, although it does provide some benefit to the building owner also. It is universally recognised that the effects of defective building (i.e., workmanship or materials not in accordance with the contract) may not show themselves until some while after the building is ostensibly complete. The effect of some defects may not show themselves for many years, as for instance in the case of foundation failure, but many will become apparent fairly shortly after the building owner takes possession or begins occupation. The absence of any provisions in the contract for dealing with these defects would leave the building owner with damages for breach of contract at common law as his only remedy. Insofar as the defects and their making good could involve him in very considerable consequential loss or expense, the builder would be extremely vulnerable. So it is provided in the building contract that where defects show themselves within a certain period, the DLP, the responsibility of the builder shall be no greater than to return to the job to put the defects right.

Under the contract, the builder has no liability for consequential loss, although the building owner does not forfeit his rights to damages for consequential loss at common law should he wish to pursue them. As an additional assurance that the builder will actually return to make good these latent defects, a small proportion of the monies due to him under the building contract, known as the 'retention fund', is held against his due performance. Were it not for these provisions, the building owner could call in any other builder to put right the defects and charge his original builder the cost of doing so. The defects liability provisions ensure that the builder has the right, for a certain period, to make good his own defects.

The most commonly selected DLP is six months, there being a general presumption that most defects will show themselves within that time or will remain concealed for very much longer. So far as monies due to the builder are being withheld, and money costs money, excessive DLPs will always be reflected in the contract sum. With the increase in mechanical services (air conditioning, and so on) in buildings, the view is commonly taken that the DLP should run for a full cycle of seasons—12 months. And the practice has grown up of writing into the contract a DLP of six months, but 12 months in respect of the M&E subcontracts and sometimes the roofing contracts as well. It is my view, and not for the first time I seem to be in a minority, that you cannot do this. If you look at the conditions of the contract in relation to the period of final measurement and the issuing of final certificates, you will see just what a tangle you will get into if the main contractor is entitled to his certificate of making good defects six months before the work of one or more of his subcontractors has even been inspected for latent defects. If you consider further that the subcontractor cannot even return to the job except under the supervision of the main contractor, the confusion and difficulties become evident. It is my advice that you can only have one DLP in a contract, although it is always possible to write in a provision for the early release of some of the main contractor's retention fund if you wish.

2.2.5.12 Liquidated and ascertained damages
An essential ingredient in any contract in law is a date for performance.
Failure to perform by the due date is a breach of contract. A simple analogy is in
the supply of goods. If a shopkeeper orders a supply of swimsuits to be delivered
by 1st June and they fail to arrive, that is a breach of contract by the
supplier—it is a fundamental breach and the question of an extension of time
will not arise. The shopkeeper required them on 1st June and by 1st July he will
have lost the opportunity to sell them. He may refuse to accept delivery and he
will also have a claim for damages for loss of profit and so on.

With building contracts, the situation is obviously more complex, and failure to
complete by the due date is not a fundamental breach, although the failure to
proceed diligently with the works may be. Failure to complete a building contract by the due date gives rise to a claim for damages in the sum of the loss
suffered by the building owner. There is always some loss, but its extent may
vary greatly between one contract and another. This presents a dilemma to a
builder tendering for a job, because in the absence of a provision for liquidated
and ascertained damages, he would have no idea whatsoever of the size of the
risk of damages that he was taking.

The provision for liquidated and ascertained damages is for the advice,
benefit, and safety of both parties to the contract. To be valid in law, it must not
include any element of 'penalty'. A building owner cannot insist on a damage
clause which in effect reads, 'If you are one week late I want £100,000'. In
legal terminology, the figure included in the contract for liquidated and
ascertained damages should be 'a true pre-estimate of loss'. Sometimes it is easy
to calculate this figure, as with a commercial development where a true pre-
estimate of the loss will be the anticipated rent. Other cases are more complex,
such as the case of a school where an education authority has arranged for an
annual intake of students and may have to make other arrangements, or the
industrial concern which has a planned programme of expansion and your
particular building may fit into the middle of it.

One item never to be forgotten when advising a client about his potential
losses arising from delay is the additional professional fees for which he will
become liable if the contract period is unduly extended. The architect is usually
the first to suffer when a contract runs behind schedule, with additional meetings, site inspections, and administrative duties. The cost can be substantial,
and it is a proper and justifiable additional charge under the standard conditions of engagement for architects. Similar conditions probably apply to the
other consultants as well. Making sure that the client includes for this item in
his assessment of his potential loss serves two purposes. First, it serves notice on
the client, if notice be needed, that you will be making an extra charge if you are
delayed by matters outside your control; and second, it ensures that the client
has the funds from which to pay those additional fees. I have heard of a recent
case where a 15-week contract actually ran for more than three times that
period, and the architect had to sue for his additional charges for the additional
service that he had to provide. The court found that he was entitled to the
money, but it immediately deprived him of it because he had failed to advise the
client that it should have been included in the calculations for liquidated and

ascertained damages. This outcome may have some appeal to admirers of symmetry, but for most of us it serves merely as a warning of the pitfalls before us.

The implications of the clause must be explained to the client and the figure agreed with him. Very often, the true pre-estimate of loss may be a very high figure and disproportionate to the contract sum. There are two ways of dealing with this. You may include the true figure, or you may write in some lesser sum. If the client requires that you write in the true figure, it should be explained to him that the builder's tenders will almost certainly include an amount of money to cover their risk in respect of potential damages. Depending on the contract, they may add in four weeks, eight weeks, or more of damages so that they have money available to take exceptional measures in order to hit the contract date, or to pay the damages if they actually incur them.

If you write in a lesser sum, then the client must understand that he will probably be out of pocket if the contractor fails to complete on time. This is usually a commercial decision, and insofar as the building is being created for the building owner's benefit, it may be quite just and proper for him voluntarily to accept the financial implications of some of the hazards of the building process. Just make sure that the advice is recorded, as is the approval of the figure.

2.2.5.13 Subcontractors

Unless you are dealing with an 'expert' client, you may have some difficulty in explaining to him the implications of employing nominated subcontractors, particularly in respect of the delays they might cause and his recourse to them if they fail to perform. The practice of nominating subcontractors is the bane of the constructing industry. Notwithstanding the attempts in the latest forms of contract to alter their status and make the main contractor fully responsible for their performance, the problems arising from the practice remain with us. With the alternative methods available in JCT 80 and the 'naming' provisions in the new Intermediate form, it is important that you explain the situation to your client and get his approval of the method of employment that will be used. Explain also the use of the employer/subcontractor agreement (the warranty) and its limitations in practice.

It is worth digressing here to draw your attention to the House of Lords decision in the case of *Junior Books* v *Veitchi*. Two extremely important points of law were established in this recent case: The first was that a building owner could sue a specialist sub-contractor in tort without going through the rigmarole of suing the main contractor and/or the architect in order to get access to him. It was held that the specialist subcontractor had a direct duty of care to those who might rely upon or be damaged by his performance.

The second point was that a damaged party could, in certain circumstances, sue in tort for the recovery of mere economic loss. In that particular case, which concerned a defective magnesium oxychloride floor, the damages awarded against the specialist subcontractor included the estimated cost of closing down the warehouse, taking out the books and racking, replacing the flooring, and reinstalling the racking and books at the end of the day. The economic loss

exceeded the cost of repairing the damage by a factor of three to one.
For architects, the significance of the first point is that if he has failed to get
a subcontractor to enter into an employer/subcontractor agreement, his client
has not necessarily forfeited his rights against him.

2.2.5.14 Possession and sectional completion

Many contracts include provisions for sectional completion, and these should
be carefully discussed with your client. The important point to note is that
sectional completion or partial occupation very often alters the conditions under
which the balance of the contract will have to be carried out. Establish in
advance what these changed conditions will be, and make sure they are fully
described in the tender documents, otherwise they may result in a very hefty
claim.
Explain to the client what is meant by practical completion. The wording of the
contract is, 'when in the opinion of the architect the building is practically
complete'. I deal with certificates of practical completion below, but it is
important to establish just what your client will consider practical completion
to be, otherwise you may find that something you and the builder consider to be
of little significance is of major importance to the client. Certifying practical
completion in these circumstances could lead to an action against you by the
client; alternatively, failure to certify practical completion could lead to action
by the builder.

2.2.5.15 Insurance

Those turgid insurance clauses! Does anybody read and understand them? If
your client has an insurance broker, obtain his advice. Most architects rely on
their quantity surveyor, but if you rely on a non–expert, you carry the burden
yourself. You need to establish that the risks are properly covered in the contract, or that your client takes out additional insurance to cover those risks
which are not included. When it comes to assessing the figures for the various
insurances, err on the high side. Particularly in respect of Clause (21.2.1) JCT
'80, Clause 19(2)(a) JCT '63, you can do no better than to envisage total
disaster. Insurance taken out in an inadequate sum is worse than no insurance
at all. Again, explain the risks to your client and obtain his approval of the sum.

2.2.5.16 Preliminaries and preambles

Every firm of quantity surveyors has its own 'standard preambles and
preliminaries'. You will usually be presented with a set of these for approval,
and the presumption is that you have read them, understood them, and agreed
that they are what you want. If they are wrong, it is your fault, and the quantity
surveyor has no responsibility in the matter at all.
The preliminaries are all those general matters applying to the site and the work
and include such matters as working space, access, foreman, working rules,
health and safety, statutory authorities, and so on. You can do no better than
prepare your own, because the action of so doing will direct and concentrate
your mind on those factors you require to be included. If you follow the
National Building Specification, you will not go far wrong.

When it comes to trade preambles, you are in effect dealing with the specification of the workmanship and materials. For some years now, in my own practice we have written our own specification, based on an office version of the National Building Specification, and that has supplanted the quantity surveyor's trade preambles. This is the only certain way of ensuring that what is measured in the bill of quantities is what you require to have built, and to the standards you wish to achieve. This has caused no little difficulty with quantity surveyors, who maintain that it puts them to additional work and that the method of description in NBS does not tie up with the standard method of measurement. It is not the fault of the architect if the quantity surveyor's standard method of measurement is not co-ordinated with the architect's standard method of specification. It is up to the quantity surveyor to measure what the architect specifies, and not the other way round. Work is proceeding apace in the preparation of guidance for the co-ordination of production information (CCPI) and we may soon be out of this dilemma. But for the moment, if you wish to avoid claims or arguments on site as to just what has been measured, write your own specification and insist that it be included in the contract as the 'trade preambles'.

If the client is faced with additional costs as a result of your inadequate specification, then he will have proper cause to seek redress from yourself.

2.2.5.17 *Query sheets*

To ensure that the architect bears full responsibility for whatever is written into the bill of quantitites, the quantity surveyor has in his office a large store of comprehensive query sheets. These will be presented to the architect at intervals during the measuring process, only too often at short notice, and they have to be completed under pressure. The quantity surveyor will state with some justification that, if only he got the information from the architect in the first place, he would not need his query sheets. Be that as it may. It is a useful precaution to ask your quantity surveyor for a complete set of his standard query sheets at the commencement of the detailed design process. They will form an excellent aide-memoire and you will be able to complete them as you go, or dispense with the need for completing them as you create your production information. Just as the quantity surveyor retains all the drawings you send through to him for the billing process, so he retains on file all those completed query sheets. If things go wrong, they are evidence against you, so make sure that you complete them correctly.

Checklist: Stages E, F and G

1 Know your own abilities and stay within them.

2 You must keep your knowledge up to date.

3 Delegation implies supervision.

4 Innovation requires extra care.

5 Control your consultants.

6 The bill of quantities is a rationalised description of *your* requirements, E&OE. *You* are responsible for what goes into it.

7 Ensure that the contract conditions are capable of fulfilment, particularly with respect to site, access, possession, and programme.

8 Have one defects liability period for the whole of the contract works.

9 Explain to your client the implications of liquidated and ascertained damages. If the figure in the contract is less than the client's 'true pre-estimate of loss', then be sure he understands his risk.

10 Seek expert advice on insurance and ensure that sums insured are adequate.

2.2.6 Stage H: Tender action
The *Architect's appointment* describes this work stage as follows:

1.17 Arrange, where relevant, for other contracts to be let prior to the contractor commencing work.

1.18 Advise on and obtain the client's approval to a list of tenderers.

1.19 Invite tenders from approved contractors; appraise and advise on tenders submitted. Alternatively, arrange for a price to be negotiated with a contractor.

2.2.6.1 Letters of intent
Because of the problems of co-ordinating the work of specialist subcontractors, it is often necessary to put subcontract works in progress before the main contract is let. The way in which this should be done is a matter of some importance, because it is not unknown for projects to be aborted or substantially delayed once the main tenders are received. The situation should be carefully

explained to your client, and his liabilities spelled out to him. If the client's pre-contract commitment to a particular subcontractor is going to be substantial, then it is essential that that subcontractor shall be named in the main contract and his acceptance by the main contractor made a condition of the tender. Otherwise you may have a situation where the main contractor, for perfectly valid reasons, refuses to enter into a subcontract, and not only is your whole programme endangered, but the client may be committed to making further payments to the unacceptable subcontractor.

There are two ways of dealing with the early commencement of subcontract works. Either the client may enter into the subcontract complete with the right to assign it all to the main contractor when appointed, or you may proceed by way of letter of intent. Letters of intent should be clear and precise and, in particular, should spell out that it is the client who has responsibility for any payments, and if there are any limitations on the financial commitment or amount of work to be undertaken in advance of the main contract. Ideally, the architect should hold an instruction from his client to issue the letter of intent, but the very minimum precaution you should take is to send your client a copy and obtain an acknowledgement of it.

Where the client enters into a subcontract with a right to assign, you should ensure that it includes provision for the possibility of the project's aborting or being delayed. The right to assign should be unconditional.

2.2.6.2 Advising on lists of tenderers

As soon as any project is submitted for planning permission, the architect will commence to receive a stream of letters from contractors, subcontractors, and suppliers, asking to be considered for some aspect or other of the project. There are various ways of dealing with this correspondence, and perhaps the safest is to consign it unceremoniously to the waste-paper basket. More likely, however, with impeccable good manners, the architect will reply in terms that indicate that at an appropriate time the correspondent will receive consideration.

A word of warning is appropriate here. If you recommend contractors to your client for inclusion in a tender list, then make sure that advice is not given negligently. To be safe, you should recommend only those firms of whom you have recent and personal experience, leaving other members of the building team to submit their own nominees and the client to add his own specific choice. If you really need to find some additional firms, then take reasonable care to check their bona fides. Certainly seek references from architects for whom they are currently working, and if you can find an architect whose name does not figure in any list the builder may have submitted to you, so much the better. On those names put forward by other members of the building team, you may only be able to advise in general terms, although it is still prudent to take up architects' references. Do not recommend firms solely on their own self-valuation or on mere hearsay, or on the contents of advertisements that you may have seen.

It is possible that some small conflict of interest may arise over this question of recommending contractors. A firm may be put forward that has a reputation for tendering low prices, but of being very claims-conscious or particularly demanding of the professional team. If you have any doubts as to the completeness of the production information, or if there is a possibility of changes of mind by the client, then it is perfectly proper to advise against the inclusion of that kind of firm. If you are simply worried about your own ability to stand up to this sort of builder, or are worried about the effect it may have on your personal profitability, then you do have a problem. If you have a good relationship with your client, he will probably understand if you explain your dilemma to him, but you cannot advise against the inclusion of a contractor simply because it is against your own interests to have him included.

2.2.6.3 Inviting and appraising tenders

On large jobs, the quantity surveyor usually has all the standard letters of invitation, forms of tender, and so on at his disposal. If you write your own, use a sound model for a guide. More important, give your intended tenders good notice of when they might expect to receive the tender documents and establish in advance that they are prepared to submit a bona-fide tender. Sending out an invitation to tender without warning is inviting refusals, or the submission of high cover prices. Alternatively, it may result in a delay to the job for which your client may hold you responsible.

When the tenders come in, they have to be opened and appraised. Contractors sometimes ask to be present at the opening of tenders, but there is no real reason why this request should be granted. It can lead to problems if, for any reason, the lowest tender proves not to be acceptable. Until a valid tender has been accepted, you should avoid giving the tenderers any information, other than an indication of where their tender sits in the list. The reason for not disclosing figures is quite simple. If the lowest tenderer discovers that he has a substantial margin on the next man, he may very well try to find reasons for bumping up his price. If the lowest tender turns out to be unacceptable, the second lowest will take similar action. Tender figures should not be released until there is a binding contract.

Where bills of quantities are used, the quantity surveyor will call for the priced bills of (probably) the two lowest tenderers, and will check them arithmetically and submit a report on them, with special reference to the general level of pricing and any idiosyncratic rates which might be written in. That report should be submitted to the architect and is not an appraisal of the tenders. The appraisal, which may include the quantity surveyor's report, should be made by the architect, and it should include any other relevant factors regarding the specific firms. While one should never invite tenders from a firm one is not prepared to recommend for a contract, it is quite correct and legitimate to take into account other factors when actually making a recommendation. The client is not bound to accept the lowest or any tender, and it is unlikely that the two lowest tenders are absolutely equal in all respects other than price. If the difference between the two lowest tenders is quite small, there is no earthly reason why you should not recommend acceptance of a tender other than the lowest. Similarly, if one tender is dramatically lower than the others, it is important that you investigate the reasons for this before recommending acceptance. 'Buying work' is only too often a short cut to bankruptcy and, notwithstanding the safeguards written into the building contract, it can seldom be in your client's interest to take a chance on that event occurring.

It is understandable that clients, having sought competitive tenders, will need very good reasons for not accepting the lowest. There are contractors of high repute who will honour their contractual commitments even at a loss. There are others who will seek to scamp the work—and this implies more rigorous site inspection. It may mean employing a clerk of works on a job that would not normally justify such an expense. It may mean more frequent inspections by the architect—again an additional expense.

Appraisal of the tenders is your opportunity to point out these matters to your client. Your job is to advise him, and he is relying on you. Though architects specifically disclaim responsibility for the contractor's working methods and so on, you cannot avoid your responsibility for not warning your client in the first instance.

Checklist: Stage H

1 Ensure that letters of intent clearly limit your client's financial commitment and provide for cancellation.

2 Name previously appointed firms in the contract documents and oblige the contractor to accept them.

3 Only recommend contractors of whom you have personal experience. Otherwise qualify your advice.

4 Appraisal of tenders should include *all* relevant matters—including the possible employment of site staff or more site staff.

2.2.7 Stage J: Project planning
The *Architect's appointment* describes this work stage as follows:

1.20   Advise the client on the appointment of the contractor and on the responsibilities of the client, contractor, and architect under the terms of the building contract; where required, prepare the building contract and arrange for it to be signed by the client and the contractor; provide production information as required by the building contract.

I am always faintly surprised that the activities defined in work stage J do not actually appear much earlier in the total process. Virtually all these activities precede the inviting of tenders, and I have dealt with them earlier in this chapter. If you are required to 'prepare the building contract', bear it in mind that the conditions in whatever standard form you are using override any other contractual requirements that have been written as amendments else-where. Amendments notified to the builder in the bill of quantities have to be actually written into the contract document itself to be valid, even though the bill of quantities becomes a contract document.

2.2.7.1 Signing the contract

Although there is an official fiction that there is only one form of contract to be signed, common practice today is for there to be two sets of contract documents and for them to be signed and exchanged by the builder and the client. Ideally, this should be carried out simultaneously, but only too often the documents are sent to the two parties for signature, and commonly one signs and returns them quite quickly while the other party sits on them. It is even possible that both parties might sit on them, and it is certainly not unknown for the works in quite major building contracts to be completed without the contract documents ever having been signed. It is a useful practice to have a third set of the contract documents neatly sealed up in an envelope in your own office. The fact that the contract has not been properly signed or exchanged is not all that significant if the actions of the parties clearly indicate their intent to sign it. In the event of a dispute, it may be a little tedious to prove the existence of the contract, but it can certainly be done, and having your own independent set is useful evidence.

2.2.7.2 Providing production information

It is the architect's responsibility to provide the builder with such drawings, specifications, instructions, and explanations as he needs in order to carry out the work in accordance with the terms of the contract. There is no evading this responsibility, and many claims against architects arise from the architect's failure to provide information on time. Usually, but not always, there would be a good defence to such a claim if only the architect had kept decent records of his activities. Changes of mind by the client and delays in giving approval are frequent causes of late information, but if they are not documented, and the client has not been advised of the consequences of his vacillation, the architect may still be held responsible. Always keep good records. Similar delays can arise on specialist subcontracts over the finalisation and approval of their details. Always ensure that your subcontract tenders, where appropriate, include clearly defined programme periods for the submission, checking, amendment, resubmission, and approval of details in their pre-site period. Lift and window contractors are notorious for delays they cause before they go into manufacture, and somehow the delay always seems to finish up as the architect's responsibility.

Checklist: Stage J

1 Amendments to the contract *must* be written into the contract.

2 Keep your own copy set of the contract documents.

3 Issue all production information in good time.

4 Ensure subcontracts include a programme for design and provision of drawings.

5 Keep impeccable records.

2.2.8 *Stage K: Operations on site*
The *Architect's appointment* describes this work stage as follows:

1.21 Administer the terms of the building contract during operations on site.

1.22 Visit the site as appropriate to inspect generally the progress and quality of the work.

1.23 With other consultants where appointed make where required periodic financial reports to the client including the effect of any variations on the construction cost.

If you use JCT '80, many of the administrative procedures are actually written into the contract. Written or not, the architect's administrative duties are manifold, detailed, and onerous. They cannot be avoided, and they have to be performed meticulously if you are not to be at risk. Building contracts are becoming increasingly complex and paper-ridden, and it has to be said that most builders detest this trend as much as architects. Therein, perhaps, lies the architect's salvation in many cases. Few contractors have either the time or the knowledge to comply with the administrative procedures laid down in the contract, and by their failure to do so, they very often forfeit their rights under the contract. Particularly is this so in respect of extensions of time. There is an obligation on the builder to notify all delays to the works. Only too commonly, builders notify only those delays for which they feel they may be entitled to an extension of time.
Frequently, builders fail to procure proper sub-contracts. When the sub-contractor causes a delay, the builder is unable to enforce the terms of the sub-contract he was told to accept, and he may thereby provide the architect with good grounds for refusing him an extension of time.
Some years ago, a contractor was pressing me for an extension of time because of delay by the nominated steelwork subcontractor. On the face of it, there was no doubt whatsoever that the steelwork had arrived late and had thereby

delayed the job. Following my usual rule, I asked the contractor to send me copies of the subcontract and all correspondence relating to it. It soon became clear that the main contractor had been in dispute with the subcontractor over his own terms of subcontract, and some six weeks after the steelwork was actually scheduled to be delivered to site, there was a letter from the sub-contractor saying, 'May we remind you that there is as yet no contract between us'! In the circumstances, it was abundantly clear that the main contractor had not taken all practical steps to ensure that the subcontractor performed on time, and he did not get his extension of time. Had the extension of time been granted simply on the apparent facts of the subcontractor's late-ness and had the client thereby forfeited his right to damages, then he would have been perfectly justified in pressing a claim against myself to make good his loss. Very many claims are made against architects because of their negligent handling of requests for extensions of time.

2.2.8.1 The obligation to interpret the contract fairly
The architect has an obligation to interpet the contract fairly between the con-tract and the client. It is the contract that he has to interpret, and not his own conscience. Extensions of time granted when, on a strict interpretation of the contract, the builder has no entitlement can result in a claim from the client. Additional payments for loss and expense awarded on no better basis than a fair appraisal of the contractor's problems may similarly, in the final event, have to be found out of the architect's own pocket. It is a hard, ruthless, and com-mercial world that we live in, and the architect is expected to know his con-tract and interpret its terms strictly. If you feel that a contractor is 'morally quite entitled' to an extension of time or additional monies, then all you can do is put the facts to your client and leave the decision to him. The parties to the contract can make whatever revisions they care to agree.
Moral dilemmas abound in the administration of the building contract, and the architect's swivel chair is too often replaced by the sharpened horns of a dilemma. At the time of the property collapse in 1974, I had just completed what had been a particularly difficult project. About a year after practical completion, the contractor submitted a heavily documented claim running to some hundreds of pages, and some tens of thousands of pounds. I knew that my client's financial position was precarious, and that a long argument over the claim would probably result in the builder receiving nothing. I also knew that to go through the claim in detail, as was my duty, would take a long while. In order to bring matters to a head, I rejected the claim in toto on the grounds that the contractor had not fulfilled some of the 'conditions precedent'. My hope was that the builder would give notice of a dispute and ask for arbitration. Instead, he put forward some counter-arguments and asked me to decide the claim.
In desperation, I resigned my appointment. The client failed to appoint a suc-cessor to me, but the builder still did not get the message and declare my client in breach of contract. Whether he would have received anything had he acted promptly, in accordance with the terms of the contract, is perhaps doubtful, but he certainly finished up with nothing, and shortly after went into liquidation. By a strict interpretation of the contract conditions, I had safeguarded my own

position. Any other course would almost certainly have rendered me liable to a claim, either from the builder or from my client.

2.2.8.2 Put it in writing

Under the building contract, all instructions have to be made or confirmed in writing. It is good practice to define at the very commencement of the contract that all instructions will be made or confirmed on an official architect's instruction form. Failure to do this may result in minutes of meetings, sundry letters, and memoranda of telephone calls being held up as valid instructions. It is a situation which can rapidly get out of control and can lead to all sorts of problems and eventual claims. If you impose a rigid discipline on yourself over architect's instructions, you will find that it pays off.

2.2.8.3 Disputes with subcontractors

It is interesting to note that you are required to administer only the terms of the building contract. By implication, it follows that you do not have to administer the terms of the multifarious subcontracts that the builder may enter into. Architects are for ever being drawn into disputes between contractors and subcontractors, laying themselves open to claims from either side in respect of their actions or decisions. The one area where you might become involved is in respect of certificates of delay (Clause 35.15.2, JCT '80, 27(d)(ii), JCT '63). If the contractor does ask for a certificate of delay against a subcontractor, then do not issue it until you have gone into the facts very carefully. If there is a likelihood of a dispute, then ensure that the subcontractor has the opportunity to put his own case before the certificate is issued. Very large amounts of money can be involved in contractor/subcontractor disputes. If you fail to issue a certificate, the main contractor may lose his rights of set-off against the subcontractor, and if you issue one which should not have been issued, and the main contractor does exercise his rights of set-off, you may find that you have lost your subcontractor, thereby damaging your client. On top of that, you can receive a claim from the subcontractor in respect of his loss. If necessary, seek your own legal advice, or ask your client to seek that advice for you.

2.2.8.4 Interim payments

The JCT forms of contract lay down very clearly what should be included in interim certificates. Essentially, it is the value of work *properly carried out* up to a date *not more than seven days prior to the certificate*. While a contractor will seldom take action against you in respect of the odd late or under-valued certificate, if you are continually negligent over the issue of certificates, you certainly render yourself liable to a claim. Money costs money, and the profit margins in most building contracts are small enough in all conscience.

But it is the 'work properly carried out' that presents the greatest danger. A quantity surveyor will measure and value what he can see. Only the architect is in a position to decide if the work has been properly carried out. Try to time your site visits to coincide as nearly as possible with the quantity surveyor's valuations, and do not be afraid to make deductions from his valuation if you know of any work which apparently has not been properly executed.

2.2.8.5 Periodic financial reports

Your client may or may not request periodic financial reports. Particularly with lay clients, there may be a presumption that the contract is actually going to cost the contract sum. Usually it is the quantity surveyor who prepares these periodic appraisals, but the architect should always vet and query them, because he may have knowledge of financial adjustments of which the quantity surveyor is as yet unaware. In the absence of any specific approval by the client, the architect's authority to certify monies is limited to the contract sum. If the contract looks like running over, then the client must be appraised of the situation in good time so that his sanction can be obtained. With small clients, there may simply not be any more money available than was in his original budget. It may be that his only course in the event of unexpected extras is to determine the contract or to cut out major items of finishes and so on. You must not assume that because the extras were inevitable and justified, the client will be able to meet the unexpected bill. Almost inevitably, in cases where the client is restricted for funds, the contingency sum will be unreasonably low, and all the elements combined make it imperative for the architect to keep a very close eye on the cost and to keep his client completely in the picture.

Checklist: Stage K Part 1

1 Know the building contract you are using and apply it meticulously.

2 Sympathy has no place in the administration of the contract.

3 Establish a firm discipline for all your administrative procedures.

4 Ensure that your client's financial commitment never exceeds the financial authority he has given you.

2.2.9 Site supervision

I am sometimes challenged for my use of the term 'site supervision', and certainly if you refer to the *Architect's appointment*, or its predecessor the 'purple booklet', nowhere will you see references to site supervision. But as my vet will tell you, you cannot make a cat bark simply by calling it a dog. Only too conscious of the limitations of an architect's site visits, the RIBA has studiously avoided a definition of just what it is that an architect is doing when he makes them.

As the *Architect's appointment* puts it: 'Visit the site as appropriate to inspect generally the progress and quality of the work'. This replaces the rather longer description in the old 'purple booklet': '. . . shall make periodic visits to the site as he considers necessary to inspect generally the progress and quality of the work and to determine in general if the work is proceeding in accordance with the contract documents'.

The new wording is at the same time both vague and precise, and it specifically places on the architect no requirement for constant supervision or frequent or regular attendance. But the purpose of the visits is clear: to establish whether the builder is fulfilling his side of the contract. In his site visits, the architect is his client's watchdog and policeman. Indeed, a client would ask, with some justice, what other purpose he has in being there at all.

In order to ascertain whether the work is being carried out generally in accordance with the terms of the contract, it is necessary to inspect the work and compare what is being provided with what is called for by the contract—in materials, in workmanship, in progress, and so on. An architect can call this inspection process what he will—in court, it will be designated 'supervision', the overseeing of the work.

There are, as yet, no cases in which the wording of the *Architect's appointment* has been tested or challenged, so we do not know whether the courts will impose a lesser onus than previously. My guess is that the site inspection process will still be dubbed 'supervision' if only because there would seem to be no other purpose in performing it.

It would be pleasant to think that the courts might recognise the limitations imposed by the undertaking to make periodic visits, but you have to bear in mind that the decision on the timing and frequency of the visits is the architect's own. It is really of little concern to the courts that the architect may have undertaken a duty that is incapable of fulfilment. In theory at least, the courts do acknowledge some limitation, and there will generally be expert evidence from both sides in a case as to whether particular aspects of defective workmanship should have been observed by an architect in the course of his site visits. But at the end of the day, the architect will commonly be held to be about one third responsible for the damage which accrues from defective workmanship. Whether or not this is reasonable, sensible, or just is mere debate; of greater importance is, what can the architect do about it?

2.2.9.1 The builder's duty to supervise

Let us first look at the contract and the builder's responsibility. It is clear that the builder undertakes to build in accordance with the drawings, specifications, and so on, and to provide all necessary plant, materials, and labour in order to do so. Clearly and incontrovertibly, the primary responsibility for supervision rests with the builder. So perhaps the architect's priority is to ensure that that responsibility is clearly written into the contract. And his first task in ascertaining that the works are being carried out in accordance with the contract should be to look at the builder's supervisory staff and insist that it is adequate both in skills and deployment.

I was recently interested to read a document showing the build-up of the rates for measured works. Having developed a long calculation to allow for all those various on-costs on a workman's time (holidays, travelling, working rule agreement and the rest), the final item was, 'Allow for supervision—5 per cent'. I am not knowledgeable enough in the ways of the building trade to interpret this precisely, but to my untutored mind it implies the employment of one non-productive supervisor for each 20 productive workmen. This is in addition to the site management set-up, which is separately priced. Usually, this 5 per cent takes the form of a working foreman, but bearing in mind the amount of building that is sub-let to specialist labour-only gangs, one is forced to question whether any effective workplace supervision is provided at all. A reputable contractor with whom I have discussed workplace supervision has expressed the view that the ratio needs to be not one to 20, but one to one.

So, is your site being properly supervised? Make it clear to the builder from the outset that you expect him to provide constant and proper supervision of the whole of the works—and that if he fails to do so, he will be in breach of contract. If you do observe bad workmanship in the course of your site visits, it is first and foremost evidence of the builder's defective supervision. I take the view that builders today are too ready to rely on the architect to perform the builder's supervisory duties for him, and they need to be forcefully reminded that the architect is not visiting the site for the builder's benefit, but for the client.

The JCT forms of contract largely encourage builders in their use of the architect as a prop and safety net, and they help to create adversarial attitudes. Too often, the builder sees his responsibility as to do no more than he can get away with. The ACA form of contract goes to much greater lengths to spell out the builder's responsibility for providing adequate skills and supervisory staff, and in that respect is a great improvement on JCT.

2.2.9.2 A form of indemnity

There is one way in which architects could protect themselves in respect of their liability for the builder's defective workmanship, and that is by obtaining an indemnity from the builder. A simple wording might be along the following lines: 'In consideration of . . . we hereby indemnify . . . [the architect] against all claims, costs, or damages which he might become legally obliged to pay in respect of any defects in the building which are adjudged to be due to workmanship or materials not being in accordance with the contract'.

The requirement for the indemnity, unless written into the contract, would need to be stated in the invitations to tender. This would serve a number of purposes. First, the contractor would be warned that he is not to rely on the architect to perform his supervisory role for him, and hopefully he would make adequate provision in his tender. He would also, with a sharp jolt, be reminded that to let him do only what he can get away with is not the intention of the contract. And it might reduce the number of claims where the architect is joined in simply for the purpose of reducing the builder's liability. As a spin-off, it might actually help to bring down the cost of architects' professional indemnity insurance.

It has been put to me that builders would vigorously contest such an indemnity becoming part of the standard terms of building contracts. For the life of me I cannot see why, and nor can those reputable builders with whom I have discussed the proposition informally.

It has to be pointed out, however, that the indemnity would be worthless if, when a claim arose, the builder was no longer in existence or was without funds. In such cases, the architect might well have to pay the entire bill for damages arising from faulty workmanship. So the possession of an indemnity does not relieve the architect of his responsibility for proper site inspection—particularly where the builder's financial stability is suspect.

2.2.9.3 *Site inspection*

How can an architect best carry out his site inspection duties to reduce his general liability in law for the shortcomings of the builder? Let us examine his position if a claim comes to court. Here he will be faced with the de facto evidence of the defective work, which clearly he has failed to observe or, having observed, has failed to do anything about. The expert retained by the claimant will state that this is a defect which would have been observed by a normally competent and conscientious architect in the course of site inspections. The best defence is to be able to demonstrate that the defective work complained about was carried out and covered up between visits, and that there was no overt evidence of it on the surface. Certainly this can be claimed where the defect is an isolated instance, and where it is not of a nature that might have demanded a special visit because of the crucial nature of that particular element of work.

2.2.9.4 *Contemporary records*

A second line of defence is to be able to demonstrate that site inspections were generally carried out conscientiously and *that the work was generally in accordance with the contract*. This, of course, is easier said than done and, years after the event, mere recollection is not very good evidence. Regrettably, what you need is contemporary records. How many architects actually record their site inspections? I don't mean those voluminous minutes of site meetings, which tend to deal with progress and queries, and in most cases merely demonstrate that the architect's time on site was mainly spent in the foreman's hut, inspecting nothing.

The greatest danger the architect faces when he visits site is that the major part of his time will be taken up with matters other than inspection of the work. Particularly is this so when the contractor is aware that defective work is being carried out and is not yet covered up. The games of hide and seek that go on on most building sites are legion and of great variety. They are played at all levels, from the workman fooling the ganger, to the site agent fooling both the architect and his own employers. We have all experienced these games, and how many times have we returned to the office from a site visit only to recollect that we haven't looked at the one item that we meant to look at? And why? Because on the way round the site, the agent drew attention to some constructional problem and the remainder of the time was spent in a debate on how to overcome it—a debate that usually entails a return to the site hut to study the drawings! The moral to be found is that you are better off making your inspections unaccompanied.

Fortunately, because at least some members of the building team can never get to site meetings before 10 am, there are usually two full hours between 8 am, when the site opens, and the commencement of the site meeting. It should be possible to make your inspection at that time, with the added advantage that the foreman will be busy with his work allocations and the men will actually be working and not away for breakfast, lunch, or tea-break.

Hide and seek

2.2.9.5 Checklists

The best advice is that site inspections should be rigidly disciplined. This entails the preparation of a checklist of items to be inspected, and a refusal to deal with other matters until every item on that checklist has been inspected. Sample checklists are published in the *Architect's job book* and elsewhere, but they should be used as a guide only in the preparations for a specific site visit. Such a checklist need not be particularly lengthy. Remember your brief: 'generally in accordance with the contract'. You are not expected to inspect everything on every occasion, but you do have to inspect sufficiently to reasonably assure yourself about the standard of work.

Special attention should always be given to a new trade commencing on site. It is in the nature of the building trade that work and workmanship do not improve with time. If a trade starts badly, the standards will only get worse. The first work you approve will become the highest standard you will be able to insist on. It is certainly easier to establish a high standard at the beginning, when condemnation of bad work will not have major repercussions on the building programme.

It goes without saying that you should know in advance just what you are looking for on your inspections. One of the drawbacks of using standard specifications such as NBS is that one is specifying great detail, often without certain knowledge of just what the item is. But there is one thing to bear in mind: if the specification refers to British Standards or Codes of Practice, then those documents, or the relevant parts of them, should be on site—otherwise the builder himself is probably not fulfilling his supervisory tasks. So it should be possible to spot-check specific items against the standard.

All the above may represent a tall order, and I comment later on the financial implications of an architect's duties in site inspections. But having carried out the inspection, how do you record it for posterity and the courts? Your checklist, provided it is adequately prepared, could have a space against each item for comments, but note-taking on site, particularly when it is raining stair-rods or you are up to your knees in mud, may not always be easy. An alternative is to take a hand recorder with you. You may find that you can consecutively record several site inspections on one tape and you then have an irrefutable and chronological record.

All this may sound extremely defensive, as indeed it is, but the jeopardy in which an architect stands in respect of site inspections cannot be overstated. I have elsewhere expressed the view that perhaps the architect should disengage himself entirely from the chore of site supervision, which too often he has neither the time nor the knowledge to perform properly. The view is not popular with some architects, who fondly believe (and they may be right) that it is only their inadequate presence that maintains any sort of standards at all. Nevertheless, I believe that supervision is still primarily the task of the builder. He has undertaken to build properly and the onus should be entirely on him to ensure that he employs the necessary skills and knowledge.

Dr W. A. Allen, much involved in building technology and most prominently an expert more often than not engaged by claimants, takes a different view. He maintains that we have moved from a traditional craft–based industry to one

which is knowledge-based. As the design has been created through the architect's knowledge, then it should follow that the architect is most likely to know
how to execute it—and the builder is right to rely on that knowledge. However, even within Dr Allen's firm, it is clearly recognised that defective workmanship may easily escape detection during site inspections, particularly if, at
some level in the contracting organisation, there is a desire to conceal it.

2.2.9.6 Opening up and testing

The remedy is—opening up! Most architects suffer from an extreme reluctance to have work opened up for inspection—not least, I suspect, because they
fear what may be disclosed. But it is the evidence disclosed by opening up that
will be brought into court and used against you. Contractually, the cost of
opening up is borne by the client, unless the work proves to be defective, so
make sure that you always have a hefty provisional sum in your contracts to be
used for opening up and testing. Once the builder realises that you have the
means and intend to use them, you will be surprised how the quality of work
will improve. The new JCT Intermediate Form provides for the builder to bear
the cost of opening up of work, where the discovery of a defect throws doubt on
the quality of work previously approved. The provision is likely to appear in
other JCT forms as they are updated.
Some items of work can be checked only by opening up, notably brickwork
and DPCs. An amusing anecdote was published in the RIBA *Journal* last year
about an architect who was very concerned that brickwork ties were not being
inserted. Yet the brickie always had a bundle of ties with him. It turned out that
the brickie always had the same bundle of ties with him, and it never
diminished in size. He kept a few loose ones with him for insertion when the
architect was actually around. Opening up a section of brickwork would have
blown that one in short order.

2.2.9.7 Dealing with defective work

Perhaps the greatest disincentive to assiduous site inspections is the hassle that
arises if work has to be taken down and re-executed. Not only may the contractor contest the architect's decision, the client himself may be unprepared
to accept the inevitable delay that will ensue. The architect may be under
pressure from both sides to accept botched solutions in the interests of speed.
If this occurs, it is vital that it be clearly recorded that it is the client's decision.
It is certainly a decision that the architect makes for himself only at very
considerable peril.
What is the position of the architect where the client insists on accepting a
standard of work that the architect knows to be defective? When the client is
an owner-occupier, the architect is probably reasonably safe to go along with
the decision after recording his protest and the implications. Different considerations apply where the client is a builder or developer and the eventual
building is for sale or rent, or whenever there are collateral agreements.
Here the position is by no means clear-cut. Certainly there is responsibility to
third parties who, in the event of damage, would be entitled to claim that they
had relied on the fact that the works had been 'supervised' by an architect.

They would, however, have to prove negligence, and that might be difficult in the face of evidence that the client had been warned of the defect. Whatever the legal position, the situation cannot fail to be a difficult one for the architect. At the very least, he should ensure that he has no direct contact with third parties, or he could become directly liable to them. Worse, if he tries to warn them of the defect, he may find himself in trouble with his client for breach of trust.

2.2.9.8 Marshalling the resources
Having established how an architect should go about fulfilling his duties of site inspection, it is perhaps worth examining whether it is feasible for him to do so. Although the architect's fee scale is recommended only, it can serve as a base from which to adduce some crude calculations. The scale makes certain presumptions, not least that the whole of the production information is complete by the time a contract commences on site, and that by that time, 75 per cent of the fee has been paid and exhausted. So the architect's total post-contract activities have to be financed out of 25 per cent of the total fee. Something has to be allowed for the defects liability period inspections and for finally putting the job to bed, so during the contract period alone, the available resource is little more than 20 per cent of the fee. If we wish to convert this cash resource into available hours, it is necessary to make assumptions about earning rates, overheads, and profit, which vary dramatically through the profession. A sophisticated central urban practice will clearly need to earn a higher rate per hour of its technical staff's time than does a very small rural practice operating from a room in the principal's home. The best guide we have—and it is not very good—is the recommended basis for charging by time: 15p per £100 of annual payroll cost. In round terms, this indicates a fee-earning level for an experienced architect of between £15 to £20 per hour. In table I, I set out the calculation of available hours for a range of different job sizes and types.

The table is worth studying and, if you belong to the small minority of architects who keep detailed cost records, it is worth carrying out some comparisons with actual jobs. Look particularly at the administrative tasks the architect has to carry out: letting subcontracts, obtaining warranties, checking sub-contractors' shop drawings, writing instructions, issuing certificates. Look at the time absorbed by site meetings and the consequent minutes. Some time, inevitably, will be spent with the client. Depending on the nature of the design and the abilities of the builder, consider the time to be spent sorting out queries, which will vary in inverse ratio to the builder's competence. Subtract the whole of that time—none of which is unavoidable—from the resource indicated by the job budget. What is left for physical inspection of the work itself? The client may fondly believe that he is paying a quarter of the fee for you to 'supervise the works'. In fact, it is more likely that rather less than 10 per cent of the fee is available for that purpose—and you don't get a lot of 'supervision' for ½ per cent of the cost of a product.

Table 1   Sample time budgets for stage K—operations on site

Basis: Recommended fee in Architect's appointment for class 3 works
20% of total fee allocated to stage K
Assumed earning potential of architect's time £15–£20 per hour

Job value		Fee implications					
New works	Works to existing	Fee (%)	Fee (£)	Weeks on site	Resource for stage K	Resource per week (£)	Resource per week (hours)
20,000		9.00	1,800	12	360	30.00	1½–2
	20,000	13.50	2,700	16	540	35.00	1¾–2½
50,000		7.80	3,900	20	780	38.00	2–2½
	50,000	11.75	5,825	16	1,175	73.00	3½–5
100,000		7.15	7,150	30	1,430	48.00	2½–3
	100,000	10.70	10,700	24	2,140	89.00	4½–6
250,000		6.45	16,125	36	3,225	90.00	4½–6
500,000		6.10	30,500	40	6,100	152.50	7½–10
1,000,000		5.90	59,000	50	11,800	236.00	12–16

Table 2 Earnings per hour on selected jobs

	Total earnings (£)	Hours	Earnings per hour (£)	Date completed or current	Remarks
Food processing factory	141,858	3,289	43.13	June '81	Fire rebuild
Major office alteration	440,000	9,607	45.80	Current	Job in stage J
Major office alteration	272,785	10,510	25.95	Current	Job not yet on site
Speculative city offices	63,222	2,590	24.41	Current	Up to stage D
Extensions and alterations to bank	23,187	1,014	22.87	April '82	Up to stage D
Speculative office refurbishment	152,024	6,831	22.25	Dec '80	
Operational warehouse	45,045	2,339	19.26	Mar '82	
Speculative office building	181,877	9,721	18.70	Current	
Four retail shops	57,016	3,169	17.99	Sept '82	Corporate image throughout
Industrial research building	37,000	2,106	17.57	Current	Partial service E F & G
Feasibility study	41,946	2,568	16.33	June '81	
Office fitting-out	73,494	4,795	15.32	April '81	Up to stage D
Mixed use development	44,080	3,005	14.67	Current	
Public utility building	14,601	1,018	14.35	July '82	
Occupational office refurbishment	43,974	3,292	13.35	June '81	Partial service E F & G
Shop and office development	28,875	2,185	13.21	Current	
Extensions to bank	85,387	7,552	11.30	Apr '81	In stage J
Extension to community centre	11,171	1,353	8.25	Aug '82	
Speculative office development	36,658	4,745	7.72	Jan '82	
Speculative office development	55,599	8,387	6.63	Feb '81	Work mainly in 1976–77
Total	1,849,799	90,076	20.53		

Note: *The above times are salaried technical staff hours only.*
Partners' time, which differs from project to project, is not included.

Checklist: Stage K Part 2

1 Insist that the contractor provides adequate workplace supervision.

2 Plan your site inspections in advance, and prepare a checklist.

3 Do not be deflected from your inspection tasks.

4 Pay special attention to newly commenced trades.

5 Periodically—and whenever any doubt exists—have completed work opened up.

6 If defects are disclosed, do not accept botched remedies. This may bring you into conflict with your client, so be prepared.

7 Keep separate records of your site inspections.

2.2.10 Stage L: Completion

Every architect knows only too well the pressures that develop as the date for completion approaches. They may come from any one or all of a number of different directions, and each source may represent a future claimant. At no time in the building process is the architect more vulnerable than when he seeks to resolve the conflicts presented by the interests of the various parties concerned with the completion of the building.

I will deal with sectional completion later, but let us look at the parties who may be involved and have an interest in a certificate of practical completion.

2.2.10.1 *The builder*

The builder wants his certificate of practical completion as early as possible, because the date will establish his liability or otherwise for liquidated and ascertained damages. If he has already passed his contract completion date, then he will start exerting pressure also for an extension of time, which would relieve him of that liability for damages. A certificate of practical completion signals the release of half his retention monies, relieves him of the responsibility for insuring the works, and sets the clock running on the defects liability period.

2.2.10.2 *Subcontractors*

At one remove, the subcontractors have the same interest as the main contractor. Although the architect has the discretion to release retentions earlier to subcontractors, often this is not done. A subcontractor who has finished his own work many months earlier may still be waiting for the release of the first tranche of retention monies. If a subcontractor has himself caused delay earlier in the contract, he may well have a very real interest in any damages which may be levied against him by the main contractor for any extensions of time which may be granted to him.

2.2.10.3 The owner

If the building is for the owner's own occupation, he may have made arrangements to move in on a certain date, or his ability to occupy and use the building may affect a whole range of other activities in his business or other affairs. At the other extreme, time may not be crucially important to him, and his concern may be for perfection of finish. If the owner is a developer, his interest in the date of practical completion may be affected by whether he has a tenant or purchaser lined up, the state of the market, or any one of a number of other considerations which have really nothing to do with the building process.

2.2.10.4 A contracting purchaser or tenant

Contracting purchasers or tenants are not parties to the building contract, but their interest in the date of practical completion is real and unarguable. It is common practice to refer to the architect's certificate of practical completion in any contract for sale or agreement for lease. The balance of purchase monies may become payable, rent or rent-free periods commence to run, responsibility for the physical fabric of the building to pass, all on the date of the certificate of practical completion.

2.2.10.5 The architect himself

The fact that practical completion will often entitle the architect to another interim fee payment will seldom affect his judgement. Regrettably, the same cannot always be said of his need to retain the goodwill of his client. However much an architect may wish to put aside his own interest, it is often at practical completion that he comes face to face with the realities of economic life.

What is the architect to do in the face of all these pressures, and how can he protect himself from potential claims? The straight answer is that he simply has to play the game by the book, record the reasons for his decisions, and be prepared to defend them against all comers. What does the book say? 'When in the opinion of the architect the building is practically complete . . .'. There have been many and conflicting views on just what is meant by 'practically complete'. Practically complete does not mean 'nearly complete'. A good definition is 'to all intents and purposes'—'complete in all respects except for some very minor matters which will not affect the owner's beneficial use'. It does not mean the day on which the client, under the pressure of other events, decides that he absolutely has to take occupation. A great deal of confusion exists over this because of the wording of clauses relating to sectional completion, where practical completion of that part is deemed to have occurred when the owner takes occupation. There is a procedure to be followed where the building owner's need to occupy the building is such that he cannot wait for the building to reach practical completion. It should be understood that the builder has an absolute right to possession of the building site until the architect issues his certificate of practical completion, and the contract provides for damages to be paid in the event of his having to retain possession beyond the contract completion date. He is under no obligation whatsoever to allow the building owner to occupy in advance of completion. The fact that the builder may be only too happy to let the building owner in, in exchange for a certificate of practical completion, is beside the point. Early occupation is a matter to be negotiated between the building owner and the contractor, and one of the matters to be discussed is relief or otherwise from damages. It does not affect the issue of a certificate of practical completion.

Perhaps the most important point to bear in mind is that if you issue a certificate of practical completion early to suit the convenience of the builder and the building owner and/or the purchaser or tenant, the defects liability period is thereby shortened and there is less time for latent defects to come to light. Anything may be agreed between the parties to a contract, but the architect is not a party to the building contract, and he is not empowered to vary its terms. Issuing certificates of practical completion with long schedules of outstanding works is not the answer to this problem; you are merely providing evidence that you have issued the certificate improperly.

I have referred earlier to those cases where there is a contracting purchaser or lessee of the building somewhere in the background. Almost inevitably, the architect owes a duty of care to this particular third party. It would be extremely unusual for the architect to be unaware of his existence, and the courts will generally assume otherwise. The third party's interest in the certificate of practical completion is probably greater than that of the original building owner/client, and he will in truth be relying on the skill, care, and integrity of the architect in the issue of the certificate. The importance of this cannot be overstressed, and no matter how willing the builder and the building owner may be to agree some sort of compromise over completion date or acceptance of substandard or incomplete work, the architect's duty is clear. If the principal parties to the contract do not like it, then they must be made to lump it. It is no use even accepting an indemnity from them on this point—the dangers are far too real.

2.2.10.6 Maintenance manuals

To me, it is one of life's mysteries that the provision of maintenance manuals is not part of the basic service, but is an optional additional service which carries with it an additional fee. There is almost no product or artefact that the consumer can buy that does not come complete with instructions for use and advice on how to maintain it. Manufacturers realised long since that their best defence against complaints about their products was the provision of operating and maintenance instructions. If that is true of a dry shaver, a washing machine, or a motorcar, then it must surely hold good for an artefact as unique and complex as a building.

The *Architect's appointment* says in Clause 1.25, 'give general guidance on maintenance'. In my view, that requirement can be fulfilled only by providing a maintenance manual. Many of the claims which arise in respect of buildings can, at least in part, be ascribed to lack of, or defective, maintenance. While it is probably true that a building owner has a responsibility for finding out how to maintain his building, nevertheless the person best able to advise him is the architect, who, with the consultants and the manufacturers and suppliers of materials and components, knows best just what is required. The need for periodic inspection is seldom understood by building owners, and failure to inspect and maintain properly very often turns minor defects into major problems, resulting in massive claims. If the building owner has been provided with correct advice on maintenance and has failed to follow it, then at least you have a good, if perhaps only partial, defence to the eventual claim. In my view, the provision of a maintenance manual should be part of the standard service, and in any event, the client should be advised in writing to commission his architect to provide one. This is something best dealt with when negotiating one's appointment, but it is certainly not too late even at the end of the job.

It has to be stated, however, that the provision of a maintenance manual opens up yet another area of risk, in that the advice in the manual has to be correct. Much of it will take the form of standard literature from manufacturers and suppliers, which reduces the burden to some extent. The Building Centre produces a very good pro-forma building maintenance manual, and this should be followed where possible.

2.2.10.7 *Final inspections*

At the end of the defects liability period, the architect has his last chance to protect his rear. It is the one occasion when the presence of the building owner or occupier is absolutely essential. He has been living in or occupying the building through the whole of the DLP, and almost certainly he will be aware of the problems which may escape an inspection by the architect, who has not been quite so involved. I am only too aware that he will probably use the occasion for nit-picking and attempting to procure the builder to make good various items of occupational damage, and it may require a certain amount of tact to persuade him that some of the items of which he is complaining are not latent defects.

However, you cannot rely on the owner or occupier simply to provide you with a list of defects. You must make your own inspection, paying particular regard to those elements of the building where defects may not be immediately evident to the owner. In particular, inspect meticulously for any signs of damp penetration. Failure of the weathertightness of buildings is arguably the greatest single source of claims against builders and architects, and even the slightest sign of water penetration can be the precursor of worse to come. Do not shirk having work opened up if need be at this stage — a trace of damp in one location may be indicative of a generic defect which in the fullness of time will occur throughout the work.

When I first entered architectural practice, the standard retention on a building contract was 10 per cent of the value, leaving 5 per cent for release at the time of final certificate. Pressure from the employing organisations on the JCT have successively reduced this 5 per cent to 2½ per cent, and now to 1½ per cent — a truly derisory sum when related to the possible cost of remedial works at the expiry of the defects liability period. If there are substantial remedial works to be carried out in relation to latent defects, there is real encouragement for the builder to walk away from his responsibilities, forfeiting his retention monies. This takes us back to the need to be careful during the periodic site inspections you make during the course of the contract.

2.2.10.8 The final certificate

No less a person than a president of the Royal Institute of British Architects has been reported as having said that he cannot remember the last time he issued a final certificate.

It may be that that particular president just had a very poor memory, or even, heaven forbid, that he was misquoted. The fact is that the signing of a final certificate is such a heavy responsibility that any architect may be forgiven for thinking long and hard before he puts his signature to that document.

In recent years, there has been some relief to architects in the interpretations that have been placed in law on the issue of a final certificate. No longer is it taken as prima-facie evidence that the whole of the works have been completed in accordance with the contract. It is, however, conclusive evidence that all those matters within the building contract which have to be carried out 'to the satisfaction of the architect' are indeed to his satisfaction. Where simple failures to meet the specification are concerned, the situation is a little more complicated, in that the architect may be relieved of responsibility if those failures could not reasonably have been detected during the course of his site inspections, take-over inspections, and final inspection. Here again is food for the lawyers and the experts. Certainly, on the issue of a final certificate, the builder will heave a sigh of relief, and the owner will assume that he is in possession of a properly constructed and eternally durable artefact.

Most standard forms of building contract lay on the architect an obligation to issue a final certificate. But that obligation is conditioned by the need for the architect to be satisfied that the whole of the works have been properly carried out. Without being unduly critical of the construction industry, it is probably true to say that these preconditions are seldom if ever met, and the architect may take a course other than actually issuing a final certificate. The particular course you adopt will probably depend on circumstances, but the range of actions may vary from leaving a nominal sum outstanding to 'conditioning' the final certificate itself.

2.2.10.9 Certificates of sectional completion

Many building contracts include provisions for the building owner to take occupational possession of one of more sections of the building before practical completion of the whole. This is particularly common in residential developments and factory projects. In housing, there is probably some provision for the architect to issue what is in effect a certificate of practical completion in respect of each house as it is taken over; essentially, this is no different from the procedure to be adopted in respect of the certificate of practical completion for an entire project. On industrial and similar work, the situation is by no means as clear. Often, the need for partial occupation will not have been envisaged at the time the contract was arranged, and even if it was envisaged and written in, it is unlikely that the full impact of the partial occupation will have been carefully considered in advance.

The wording in the JCT contract is, 'if with the consent of the builder . . .'. The builder's consent is important, because he is losing part of his possession of the site. It may seriously affect his working method and costings. Even if your client is champing at the bit and has an urgent need to take over the building, he still requires the builder's consent, and if he goes in without it, he will be in breach of contract. Sectional completion can give rise to all sorts of claims from the contractor, and if you have not properly advised your client of the possibility of these claims, then he may seek reimbursement from you, his luckless architect. Nevertheless, even with the builder's consent, a part of a building does not need to be 'practically complete' for the building owner to begin to occupy and use it. You should always agree with the builder in advance what is to be done about the outstanding works, although there is little you can do about the defects liability period, which will commence to run as soon as the building owner takes up occupation or possession. One final point: do not forget to remind your client of his responsibility for insuring that part of the building which he has taken over.

2.2.10.10 Archives

The question is often asked, 'What, when the job is finished, should be retained as archives and for how long?'. The general practice is to keep almost everything for almost ever, which creates a storage problem if nothing worse. As I understand the legal position, most of those papers you accumulate during the course of a project belong not to you, but to your client. An architect's employment is that of an agent, and all his acts are carried out on behalf of his client. Accordingly, all the documents — not only forms of contract and statutory consents — belong to the client and are retained by the architect only for safekeeping.

The sort of documents that do not belong to the client are your correspondence with him on your own appointment, correspondence with directly employed consultants, and your own working papers and preliminary development sketches.

The current practice of retaining all documents seems to have developed from the dilemma presented to an architect by this question of ownership. While, presumably, an architect could simply bundle up all the files and drawings and send them to his client, together with the final certificate, there can be few with the confidence to adopt this course. In every architect's files are letters that, at the very least, could precipitate embarrassing questions if subjected to the scrutiny of a hostile reader.

Similarly, requesting a client's permission to destroy the documents is not likely to bring a favourable response. Keeping the documents and saying nothing is the easiest way out. Once the client has ceased to exist — for example, by company liquidation — you have greater freedom of choice but still need to remember those potential third party claimants.

Retaining all the documentation on projects does present a storage problem. Some firms deal with this by 'thinning the files' before consigning them to the archives. While technically even those insignficant standard responses should be retained, the real danger is in having to decide in advance just what is, or is not, of significance — an almost impossible task, and a very time-consuming one, which generally has to be carried out by a partner.

In my own firm, we decided many years ago to microfilm all our records, destroying the originals with the exception of contracts and statutory consents. There is a cost involved, but this is more than outweighed by the saving in partners' time in going through the files to 'thin' them. There are other advantages — not least that once a document is on a reel of microfilm, it cannot become 'lost' if at some later date it has to be referred to. Also, there can be little dispute that records disclosed on 'discovery' in a court case are complete. If you do decide to microfilm, you should go the whole hog and have a duplicate film retained in a safe place or by the microprocessors. Theoretically, you should obtain your client's permission to microfilm his documents, but this will seldom be refused. Surprisingly, there is little legal formality in England in 'proving' microfilms as evidence in court: they seem to be accepted as a matter of course. In some countries, micro-records have to be 'sworn' at the time they are created if they are to be acceptable in the courts.

Finally, a word of warning. Satisfy yourself of the efficiency of the micro-filmers before destroying the originals. Nothing can be worse than discovering later that you have a blank or illegible roll of film!

Checklist: Stage L

1 The 'opinion of the architect' is paramount in deciding practical completion.

2 Have regard to your duty to third parties.

3 A maintenance manual can be a good insurance — but make sure it is correct.

4 Don't be afraid to order 'opening up' at final inspection if you have evidence of defect.

5 Do not issue a final certificate if you have any reason to doubt that the work has been properly executed.

6 Ensure that you have the builder's consent (in writing) before you let your client take partial possession, and don't forget to advise your client of his responsibility to insure.

7 It is your decision to keep or destroy the records. If you keep them, keep them all. If you opt to destroy, then let the client have anything that does not belong to you — contracts, consents, and agreements. Technically, as you are acting as the client's agent, nearly all the documents, including correspondence, belong to him, so if you do decide to destroy, you should seek his permission first.

2.3 Other services

Now that I have examined in detail the nature of the basic service most commonly provided by architects in the building process, it might be thought that the architect had taken upon himself a sufficient burden. The range of knowledge and skill required of him is greater than that in any other profession or in any other activity in the construction industry, and the scope provided to the architect for rendering himself liable for damages to other parties is almost boundless. I hope that I have been able to indicate those areas in which special care has to be exercised and, in particular, the need not to undertake any activities where you have any doubts at all as to your competence and ability to deal with them properly.

However, the presumed omniscience of the architect's profession knows no limits, and the *Architect's appointment* lists in Part 2 those other 'services which may be provided by the architect to augment the preliminary and basic services . . . The list of services so described is not exhaustive'. Some 44 different types of activity are listed, not including those which are more normally provided by specialist consultants.

Many of these services are those commonly occurring during the course of a normal project for which one is supplying the basic service, and, to some extent, they are included in the list of additional services in order that they shall qualify for additional fees, or be properly taken into account when one is negotiating an overall fee for the project. Mostly, the implications of these additional services in respect of liability have already been covered generally within the preceding part of this book, but some of them give rise to special aspects of risk or liability and merit special comment. Others are quite specialised in nature and will be carried out only by architects who have developed a particular expertise. The risks involved in those specialisms are beyond the scope of this book and beyond my ability to comment. Let us look at the more common other services that do give rise to special risks.

2.3.1 Building sites

2.1   Advise on the selection and suitability of sites; conduct negotiations concerned with sites and buildings. (*Architect's appointment*)

It is every architect's dream that his client will actually ask him to advise on the selection of a building site before he embarks on a project. This happens all too rarely. Generally, the architect comes on the scene to be presented with a site which either has been long in the ownership of the client, or has already been acquired with or without the advice and assistance of an estate agent. Frequently, because the client has insufficient knowledge of his own accommodation problem and its probable solution, the site may have inherent defects which prejudice the best solution. So if the architect is invited to advise on the suitability of a site yet to be acquired, it is an opportunity with great potential for good, and one which is not to be taken lightly.

It must be assumed that, if a client has had the good sense to come to his architect for advice on the suitability and selection of a site, it is because he recognises the special input that the architect has to contribute and that he is not concerned simply with the bearing capacity of the soil. It follows that the architect may need to do considerable preliminary work to establish the physical criteria of the most suitable site. The choice of site will usually be limited, and seldom will the recommended site be ideal. It may be necessary to carry out feasibility designs to establish the suitability of the site, and the cost implications of this should be explained to the client. Other matters which should be taken into consideration have already been dealt with under site appraisal, and they assume very great relevance if, as a result of your advice, the client goes ahead and purchases an expensive piece of land.

Architects often find themselves willy-nilly conducting negotiations concerned with sites and buildings. Under the newly relaxed Code of the RIBA, there is nothing to prevent an architect from acting as an estate agent, but how he should go about it is beyond the scope of this book.

2.3.2 Structural surveys

The risks inherent in carrying out structural surveys are so well known and documented that there is little point in recounting them here. For a certainty, the findings of the courts as to what constitutes negligence in structural surveys place such an onus on the surveyor that he takes his professional life in his hands every time he surveys a building. Regrettably, the only way that you can provide yourself with a modicum of safety is to so bespatter your survey report with conditions and caveats that it is little better than worthless. Many firms, even firms of surveyors, will not touch house surveys at all, and those that do are continually increasing their fees for the service in order to cover their risk.

Your insurance policy will set out in detail a disclaimer clause to be included in all structural survey reports. Make sure you use the precise wording. Your policy may also lay down just who may be permitted to carry out structural surveys. If you use unqualified and/or inexperienced staff, you will not have the strength of your insurance company behind you.

Just remember, the purchaser may be investing the whole of his future life savings on the basis of your advice that the building is sound. Whatever you may tell him, he believes that a clean survey report is a lifetime guarantee. So on his behalf and your own, you just cannot be too careful. Perhaps the greatest area of risk is the survey made for a friend, very often without any charge at all. The fact that you have made no charge is absolutely no defence in law if your friend suffers as a result of your advice.

If you are going to do structural surveys, then do them properly. Prepare a good checklist of all the items you will want to inspect, and make sure that you have the ability to inspect them properly. If you require the assistance of a builder for carrying out a drains test, or ladders for access to a loft, then make sure that they will be available while you are on site. If there are items on your checklist which you would have liked to inspect but were unable to do so, then make sure you mention this in your report. If you see signs of trouble, the extent of which you are unable to determine on first inspection, then recommend a fuller and more detailed inspection of that particular aspect. More particularly, if you are inspecting an occupied property, do not take too much notice of explanations that the vendor might give you about that particular problem.

I am sure that everybody can tell a similar story, but I am reminded of a house survey that I carried out as a very young architect for a friend of a relation and for a very low fee. There were definite signs of dampness in the ground floor, but the owner, an architect of some repute, assured me that it had all been attended to. Even as a young architect, I was not going to fall for that one, so in my report I recommended that the purchaser had a full inspection made by one of the disinfestation companies. A few days later, I was presented with a report which had been obtained from a disinfestation firm by the vendor's agent. I was not happy with it, and I pleaded with the purchaser to have a further inspection made. Anxious to purchase the house, he ignored my advice, accepted a token reduction in the price, and went ahead with the purchase. Two months later, I was awakened by an early morning phone call and a piteous tale from the purchaser, who had now discovered that he had to replace the whole of the ground-floor slab. For reasons which to this day I still do not understand, I found myself 'supervising' the remedial work for no charge. The client certainly had no case for suing me, because of the warnings I had given him in writing. But the story does demonstrate that with surveys you just cannot be too careful.

2.3.2.1 Building society surveys
It is, of course, possible today not to carry out a structural survey and still be held responsible by a purchaser for a subsequent structural failure in a house. This has arisen because of the case brought by a Mr Yiannis against a surveyor commissioned by a building society to provide it with a valuation survey. The report included the general disclaimer that it was for the benefit of the building society only and, as it happened in that particular case, Mr Yiannis, the purchaser, did not even see it. It was held in court, however, that because he knew that his building society mortgage was dependent on a satisfactory survey report, he had in effect relied on that report in deciding to proceed with the purchase. He was awarded damages against the surveyor in respect of the subsequent failure of his foundations on the grounds of the surveyor's negligence. The principle of tort had been interpreted to lay upon the surveyor acting for the building society a duty of care towards the subsequent purchaser, because it was within his reasonable contemplation that the subsequent purchaser would be relying on the outcome of his survey. Granted, the survey was only for a valuation, but clearly the house would not have the value ascribed to it if it had defective foundations. It is an interesting piece of logic and has caused a lot of heavy thinking among people who habitually carry out surveys for building societies.

Partly as a result of that case, and partly because of the expense to house purchasers of paying for a building society survey and then having their own survey carried out in addition, the practice is spreading of building societies making available to purchasers a limited form of survey report, which covers the main structural features of a property but does not comment on decorative condition and minor matters. Such a survey generally takes the form of a completed pro-forma and the surveys are very often carried out by architects. If you are undertaking this type of survey, then have the pro-forma checked to ensure that you are not committing yourself to a greater degree of liability than you anticipate. The RIBA has prepared a suitable pro-forma for this type of limited survey.

2.3.3 Other types of surveys and investigations

There are altogether 12 different types of surveys or investigations listed under 'other services'. Almost all of them imply some sort of specialist knowledge on the part of the architect, and the standard of service that you provide will at any later time be judged on the presumption that you did have that specialised expertise. It is all too easy to undertake many of these additional services because they appear to be quite simple and straightforward, but the reverse may be true when you actually delve a little deeper. If you find that you are getting out of your depth, the only sensible thing to do is to go back to your client and to insist that he employs a specialist. More often than not, the architect's best role in these cases is merely to advise on the selection of the most appropriate expert or the best method of going about the task.

Services in respect of leased or rented property are commonly undertaken by archtitects, either in the form of surveys and advice prior to entering into a lease, or in preparing or contesting schedules of dilapidations on the expiry of a lease or at some other time. The cardinal rule in undertaking this sort of service is to insist on having a copy of the lease. No two leases are alike, and commonly used expressions such as 'full repairing and insuring' or 'internal repairing only' can be extremely misleading and will be written and interpreted differently in the documentation. Make sure that you fully understand the implications of the lease. A common pitfall is the lease which apparently has an internal repairing covenant only, but places on the tenant, through the medium of a service charge, responsibilities for repairs to the main structure. It may be very tedious when your client is only taking a lease of 1000ft. of space, but the structural condition of the entire 50,000ft. of the building is his concern to at least 2 per cent of the extent. His space may be on the ground floor, but he still carries a liability for 2 per cent of the cost of replacing the roof, which may be in the last stages of dilapidation.

Development services and design services are fairly straightforward, and the risks and the expertise necessary are all self-evident. Cost estimating and financial advisory services, item 2.25 to 2.28, cover a useful area of recolonisation in a field more usually resigned to the quantity surveyor. If you feel confident to do it, by all means go ahead. Judging by the apparent immunity of quantity surveyors to claims for negligence, there would not appear to be any major areas of risk. There are, however, a few points of which you should take note.

When advising on the cost of reinstatement to be written into a fire-insurance policy, you should always look at the terms of the policy itself. Almost certainly, the terms of the policy will require that the figure written in is the total figure for complete reinstatement, including the removal of fire-damaged debris. You may believe that works below ground will not be harmed by a fire and that your client will be able to rebuild off the existing foundations. Be that as it may, the insurers will almost certainly want to see the full cost as the sum insured. It is on that basis that they assess the premium. Furthermore, in assessing the figure, you should allow for inflation, assuming that the property will not be destroyed until the last day of the annual policy into which the figure is going to be written, and that preparation for rebuilding may increase the cost by another year of inflation.

Submitting and negotiating claims following damage by fire or other causes requires some knowledge and care. If it is a major claim, it is far better dealt with by professional fire assessors and loss adjusters, and my advice would be to keep well clear of it, if only because the specialist experts will probably do a better job for your client.

2.3.4 Applications for grants

Making applications for, and conducting negotiations in connection with local authority, government or other grants has its pitfalls. In its desire to open up the field of small works for its members, the RIBA has widely publicised the fact that this is a service architects can provide. If this is a field in which you wish to operate, then make sure that you know all the rules. The clients are almost invariably small house-owners or small-time developers, and they rely very much on obtaining their grants either to do the work at all, or to make it worth doing. If they find that they have forfeited their grant because of the failure of their architect to comply with the rules or to meet the submission dates, they tend to become a little antagonistic — and who can blame them?

2.3.5 Negotiations

There are two areas of risk here, notably those associated with planning appeals, 2.30, and the rights and responsibilities of owners or lessees, 2.34.

2.3.5.1 Planning appeals

Whatever may have been the intention behind the Planning Act, and regardless of whatever is written in the *Notes for appellants* issued by the Department of the Environment, planning appeals are usually best dealt with by specialists and experts. While losing a planning appeal may not be the end of the world (because the owner usually will have the right to make a new application and start again from the beginning), it can be a very costly business, both directly and because of the time involved. The most important decision that has to be made when you receive a planning refusal, or a permission with unacceptable conditions, is whether to appeal on written representations or to request a public inquiry. If the decision is to go for a public inquiry, then the matter simply has to be dealt with by a specialist lawyer. The standard of advocacy and legal argument at public inquiries is at least equal to that in the High Court, and I know of no architect who is equipped to undertake that task. Even written representations require considerable experience, and you should bear in mind that facing you is the local planning authority, which is doing this sort of thing all the time. But first and last, keep in view the expiry date of your client's right to appeal. If your appeal is thrown out because it is out of time, your client will have good grounds for a claim against you, to which there will probably be no defence. In passing — the latest edition of *Notes for appellants* incorrectly states that an appeal has to be lodged within six months of the date of the planning authority's decision. This is erroneous: you have six months from *receipt* of the decision.

2.3.5.2 Rights of owners and lessees

Most architects have a good working knowledge of the rights of building owners and are usually quite good at negotiating party wall awards and so on. Valuing rights of light and their extinction or diminution is another matter, and again unless you have a specialist knowledge and experience, it is best left to the experts.

2.3.6 Administration and management of building projects

'2.37 Provide site staff for frequent or constant inspection of the works.' This has been mostly dealt with under site supervision (above) and partial service (below). The most important thing from the architect's point of view is to make sure that the terms under which he undertakes frequent or constant inspection do not imply any responsibility for the perfection of the finished product. Avoid any terms of engagement to the effect that you will 'provide inspection services as necessary to *ensure* the proper completion of the work'. I read with wry amusement the description in the *Architect's appointment* under the heading 'Project management' (2.38). I recognise it as the task which architects habitually undertake as their basic service under a normal commission. In the experience of most architects, project management consists of the interposition between himself and his client of a designated project manager, whose main function appears to be no more than to vet the various consultants' fee accounts. The conventional wisdom is that architects are bad managers, and it is refreshing to see their insitute putting forward project management as a discipline in its own right that can be provided by architects. It is, of course, possible for an architect to be a project manager on a project for which he is not the architect. Therein perhaps lies the greatest area of risk, because I know of no architect who does not think that he can design a building or solve an accommodation problem rather better than any of his fellow architects. So inevitably there will be a temptation to interfere with the project architect. From everything else that has been written in this book, the budding project manager should know better than to embark on that course. The essence of project management is to ensure that there is no lessening of the responsibility of any of the individual people, firms, or companies appointed by him, particularly at the risk of his own exposure to claims.

Separate trade contracts, 2.40, and direct labour, 2.41, are two types of service where the hard line between providing a professional service and acting as a contractor is becoming somewhat blurred. Particularly in view of the changes in the Code of Conduct which permit an architect to act as a contractor, you should be particularly careful in the drafting of your terms of appointment. In particular, you should always ensure that the providers of services, labour, and materials are all employed directly by your client, and if he does not want 'to be bothered with all that nonsense', set up a special client's account at the bank, to be put and maintained in credit by your client, from which all payments will be made.

The risks inherent in this kind of activity fall into two categories: The danger that your professional identity will become submerged, and you will appear to the client as the provider of the building; and that you will by inadvertence become a design/builder warranting 'fitness for purpose'.

Checklist: Other services

1 If an additional service demands an expertise that you do not have, leave it alone.

2 Advice on suitability of sites may entail substantial feasibility studies. If you advise on the suitability of the site, you cannot complain later about the constraints it imposes.

3 Read your professional indemnity policy before embarking on structural surveys.

4 Do structural surveys fully or leave them alone.

5 If surveying for a building society, remember your responsibility to the purchaser.

6 When surveying for a landlord or a tenant, insist on having a copy of the lease.

7 When estimating costs of reinstatement for insurance, project costs forward two years.

8 When obtaining grants for clients, learn the rules thoroughly so that you do not inadvertently disqualify your client.

9 Planning appeals are not as easy as the Department of the Environment's *Notes for appellants* indicate. Whatever you do, don't miss the latest date for submission.

10 If you undertake project management, then manage — do not try to do anybody else's work for them: you may take on their liability.

11 If you administer separate trade contracts, ensure that your own professional role is clearly defined and evident. Never pay workmen out of your general practice account.

2.4 Partial services

While a common view of the architect is of a man who, taking his client's problem to his bosom, sees it through thick and thin to the occupation of the completed building, the reality is often something very different. What is known as 'partial service' has always been recognised in the architect's terms of engagement, and latterly in the *Architect's appointment*. There are many variants on the theme of partial service, and it is worth looking at them in some detail to distinguish their salient features and the extra hazards they present to those who carry them out.

Some types of partial service present no increased hazard to the architect, such as a commission to obtain an outline planning consent. Even if he has inadvertently made a defective application, and the consent subsequently proves to be invalid, he will be no worse off than if the same result had eventuated after he had seen the job through to completion. By far the greatest hazard arises when an architect is commissioned to carry out part only of the basic service set out in the *Architect's appointment*, where it is known that a building will be constructed.

Partial service may be categorised as 'vertical' or 'lateral'. The first category includes all those commissions where the architect either commences after the beginning of the project, or finishes before the end. Most common is perhaps the 'town planning and building regulations' instruction, particularly prevalent in housing and industrial work. I will return to this.

Less common, but in some ways even more hazardous, is the 'lateral' variety, where the client provides part of the service himself in one or more stages of the design and construction process. Usually, this will be because the client maintains his own in-house experts and only too often sees in them a way of justifying a reduction in the architect's fees. In all probability, the architect is better off where the contribution of the client's architect's department is no more than a fiction. The real dangers arise when that department's input is real and measurable, because the architect may find in the event of failure that he has assumed responsibility for the work of others.

But I will deal first with the 'vertical' variety, because experience shows that it is in this area that architects most often come croppers.

The principal types of vertical partial services are as follows:

1 To obtain town planning approval in order to establish the value of a site for purposes of sale.

2 To obtain town planning and building regulations approval for either a client who will then find his own builder or build himself with or without direct labour; or for a builder/developer usually, but not always, in the speculative housing field.

3 To provide production information for a client who has his own design organisation; this may or may not follow through to supervising the contract.

4 Supervision only, which is most common where a purchaser is buying a new building 'off the plans' and requires a watchdog; a variant is where he is obtaining a package-deal building.

2.4.1 Outline planning permission
As I wrote earlier, category 1 presents little in the way of additional risk, and
you can make doubly sure of the position by boldly inscribing on the drawings,
'These drawings are for the purpose of a planning application only and must
not be used for the purposes of building'.

2.4.2 Town planning and building regulations
The second category is a positive deathtrap. Proceed with the greatest caution.
Some of the most outraged letters from practitioners that I have seen start, 'In
1955 (or some such date) I obtained town planning and byelaw consent for a
friend who wanted to build himself a house'. Then follows what is virtually a
standard catalogue: the £50 fee — the ladder-and-barrow local handyman or
DIY enthusiast — the new owner in 1965 — the drought in 1976 — the cracking and subsidence — and a claim for £10,000 or £20,000 or more. The
number of houses that were designed in the 1950s for £50 or £100 and always for
a friend is positively mind-boggling. And when you recall (those of you who
are old enough) that steel was on licence and virtually unobtainable, and you
could use only 1.6 standards of timber per house, it is not surprising that after
20 or 30 years, things have gone wrong. Houses were built on tips, on made
ground, and on filled bomb craters. The drawings always carried the note,
'foundations to the approval of the building inspector'. It was common
practice and, with the benefit of hindsight, it was negligent. Come to think of
it, the calibre of some building inspectors in the 1950s was not such as to inspire
the deepest confidence. These cases, and there truly are very many of them,
illustrate the greatest danger with this kind of partial service — the architect
does *not* visit the site during the construction, and so he does not have the
opportunity to catch the clanger before it hits the ground. Trusting individual
that he is, he is relying on somebody else to do that for him, while they, ignorant
in the main, are relying on his professional skill in the drawings, which
prominently display the rubber stamp of the local authority — 'Approved'.
The building inspector to whose approval the foundations were to be constructed may have been no more than a pimpled youth — or may not have
visited the site at all!
During the 1960s, the RIBA was so anxious for its members to get into the
booming housing market, seemingly at any price, that it promulgated a special
fee scale for what it termed 'limited service for estate developers'. The fee was to
be based on the selling price of the house! No attempt was made to relate it to
the service the architect had to provide, only to the price the house would fetch
on completion. The service included estate layout, and town planning and
byelaw approvals. The presumption was that the builder/developer, 'knowing
his own trade', had no need of working drawings or specifications, and for the
sake of his reputation would ensure that the work was properly carried out.
I have an interesting case on file, where the 'builder' was one man with a part-
time secretary and the 'site foreman' was a self-employed labour-only carpenter
subcontractor. Building did not commence until some six years after the architect had completed his 'service' and had severed all contact with his builder/
client. The site was graded to slopes different from those shown on the approval

drawings, but foundation levels were not adjusted. The site flooded regularly during and after construction. Eventually, the foundations of some of the houses failed, and the failure was adjudged to be caused by tree roots from adjacent property. Writs were issued against the architect, the builder (who promptly went into liquidation), the local authority, and the adjoining owner.

The case was settled 'on the steps of the court' for not too much money, with the architect's insurers picking up 20 per cent of the bill, to which the architect contributed his excess. In the circumstances, not too bad, you might think. But it so happened that the luckless architect had given a 'limited service' to this particular jerrybuilder for some two or three hundred houses. You can imagine his horror when, applying to renew his insurance, he was told that in respect of all those houses, there would be an imposed excess of £7,500 for each and every claim. He is left with an uninsured exposure of more than £2,000,000! There is a lesson here which does not rightly fall within this chapter: if your insurers are prepared to settle for a modest sum when you believe you have a good case to defend, before you agree, check what the effect will be on renewal of your policy. However, the true moral of this tale — and it is borne out in many court judgements — is that a small fee (or no fee at all) does not relieve a professional man of his responsibilities to third parties. No matter that your client will not heed your warnings — render them in writing none the less. State the basis on which the foundations have been designed and the assumed ground conditions. Advise the builder to employ an engineer to check the ground conditions, and have the foundations redesigned if they differ from the assumptions. And so on.

2.4.3 Production information

The third category — taking over somebody else's design and creating the production information — presents a whole new panorama of risk. It is simple enough to frame an agreement wherein you absolve yourself from any responsibility for the design. That is *before* you start on the detailed drawings. The problems arise when the 'design' proves to be incapable of translation into a sensible, buildable set of drawings because, if you alter the design in any way, your absolution has gone out of the window. There is no alternative to referring the 'design' problem back to the designers and insisting that they solve it. Solve it yourself, and obtain the designer's approval, and all you have achieved is a share of the burden of liability.

If you are not going to be involved in the construction process, you are in the same position as the category 2 architect when it comes to designing work below ground. Clearly set out all the caveats and warnings.

A frequently overlooked aspect of work stages E, F, and G partial service, is the anomaly created by the traditional staging of fee payments. It has always been recognised that the architect's stage payments are 'front-loaded' — i.e., that the percentages of the total fee payable for stages C and D are high in relation to the actual work. To some extent, this is to compensate the architect for the greater input of skill and original thought required in the conceptual design, but also the loading serves to finance the following process (stages E, F, and G). What this means in practice is that if an architect agrees 'the appropriate stage fee for stages E, F, and G', he is forgoing part of the true cost of the work. In effect, he is on a cut fee from the outset. But that is not the end of the story. Taking over somebody else's design actually increases the workload, in that the architect has to familiarise himself with a design — a process that, in the full basic service, is automatic during the development of the design. So the temptation may arise to bypass some of the to-ing and fro-ing on the design changes, exposing the architect to future risks.

Let me reiterate: when undertaking a partial service, insist on an agreement that quite clearly sets out the respective responsibilities and roles of the parties, and more particularly, as the job progresses, record any deviations or departures from it. Try to ensure that you obtain the correct fee for the commission, and explain to your client the reasons for what appears to be an additional charge, and for a punctilious attention to administrative detail. After all, the client usually prepares this kind of set-up for reasons that are totally beneficial to him. You may want the work quite badly — but not at the expense of your future security.

2.4.4 Supervision

Finally, in the vertical partial services, we come to supervision. Here, inevitably, we depart radically from anything written in the *Architect's appointment*. Your client is employing you for one reason and one reason only: to ensure that the work is carried out in accordance with the contract! However vague, cryptic, or discursive may be the description of site inspections in the *Architect's appointment*, your client expects you to carry out whatever inspections are necessary to ensure that he is getting his money's worth and that he will have a sound job at the end of the day. Before undertaking a service of this nature, establish clearly the conditions under which you will have to execute it. I am assuming that we are not dealing with one of the standard forms of contract but, as is more usual, some lesser document, often one devised by the builder himself entirely for his own convenience, protection, and commercial benefit.

Establish clearly just what rights of inspection are written into the building contract and whether there are any sanctions that can be applied if you observe bad work or materials. Probably there will be none, and your course of action will be limited to reporting to your client. If that is the case, then this is what you should do — in writing! Anything you may say to the builder will be of no effect, except to give the builder an excuse for putting part of the blame for his breaches of contract on your shoulders. Whatever you do, don't suggest alterations or amendments, or you will acquire a design liability. Don't undertake to ensure that the work will be carried out properly. Even an architect with full powers under a JCT or similar contract should never do this.

In these situations, both drawings and specifications tend to be minimal. Much of your inspection will be devoted to establishing whether the work complies with accepted good practice — always ground fruitful for dispute and generally related to a level of cost. It should be made clear to both your client and the builder that the responsibility for building properly is the builder's. The builder cannot rely in any way on your inspections. Nor, for that matter, can the client, if his contract permits him no remedy if defective work is reported to him.

When making your agreement with your client, define, so far as possible, what is expected in terms of time to be expended or the number of visits. It is very common for a building contract to provide for inspection at set stages, usually to coincide with interim payments. If you are only making three or four visits, then quite clearly you cannot be expected to have seen all the work that has taken place between stages. This kind of intermittent inspection is not really supervision at all, particularly if you have no power to order the opening up of work. A useful protection is to snap off a roll of film on this kind of visit.

However, with all the caveats you may write into your appointment, periodic inspections still have to be carried out carefully, perhaps more carefully than if you had been observing the work at shorter intervals. If defects do disclose themselves later, the first person the client will look to is yourself. What else would you expect when the prevention of defective work was the only reason he had for employing you? Bearing in mind the toothless nature of your role, you may consider this unreasonable: 'If you can't stand the heat, get out of the kitchen'.

2.4.5 Taking over from another architect

It sometimes happens that an architect is asked to take over from another architect who has been concerned with a conventional project. This may occur for many reasons, the two most common being the death of the previous architect or a disagreement between architect and client. I don't propose to discuss the commercial hazards of the latter circumstances beyond saying that before you accept the commission, try to find out, from both sides if possible, the reason for the disagreement.

The main professional danger lies in what may have happened in the period immediately before the transfer of appointment — the things that may have gone wrong and the actions which may not have been taken at the appropriate time. Try to ensure that whatever fee arrangement you agree allows for the time you will spend familiarising yourself with the project, correcting previous errors, and so on. Too often, architects take over a project on the basis of the original ad-valorem fee less a proportion deducted in respect of the work previously carried out and paid for. It really does not work like that — and any service undertaken for an inadequate fee presents the possibility of enhanced risk.

Some years ago, my own practice was asked by a local authority to take over a project which had been held up by one of the periodic government expenditure cuts just before it went out to tender. Ostensibly it was fully drawn. Fortunately, we agreed a familiarisation fee, a time charge for drawing work, and an ad-valorem fee for stage J. Only a few years had elapsed since the drawings had been done, but in the interim, part FF of the Building Regulations had been introduced, cold–bridging had been discovered, and certain space and amenity standards had changed. We finished up virtually re-drawing the entire job, and the final cost was greater than the scale fee we would have required for a full appointment. You do not need to look too deeply to detect the moral in this tale.

That particular project was a partial service that effectively overlapped into the 'lateral' category. Certainly, the final design was a combined effort by ourselves and the local authority architect's department. Working for local authorities, health authorities, nationalised industries, and corporations with in-house architects or engineers gives rise to a situation which might be considered unfair and undesirable. The power and the in–house expertise of the commissioning authority often serve to submerge the independent practitioner's own professional judgement. Very often, solutions are adopted which are either combined efforts or entirely the brain-child of the clients own in–house experts. Unless there is a clear agreement to the contrary, the outside architect accepts total responsibility. Furthermore, if anything goes wrong, the in–house architects who were involved in the matter are now on the other side. Little can be done to remedy this situation, other than to maintain your professional judgement at all times. If the commissioning authority is, in effect, acting as a consultant to you, then let it be clearly stated in the agreement that this is so — and you are entitled to rely on their expertise in these circumstances. If, on the other hand, they are simply giving you an informed brief, the buck stops on your desk!

2.4.6 Partial service is always for the client's benefit
A point you should always bear in mind is that it is seldom the architect who proposes a commission for partial service. Either for his own convenience, or more probably to save money, it is the client who makes the suggestion. The client does not usually understand the full implication of what he is suggesting, so it is always worth going to the time and trouble of explaining it to him fully. Prepare, in advance if you can, a letter or paper setting out the limits of your responsibility and the procedures you will want followed. Certainly and always, have them understood and accepted before you undertake any commitment. You will always be in a weak position if you try to lay down conditions after you have started work. I make a particular point of this because that admirable document, the *Architect's appointment*, is all written around the presumption of a full service. In partial service, the rules change very considerably. An exchange of letters simply referring to the *Architect's appointment* can lead you into a peck of trouble.
Tie up the fee basis as carefully as you can. Partial service creates additional time demands compared to full service and, with the boundaries less well defined, you can find yourself doing far more than you bargained for, with no recompense. If the client finds he is saving less than he thought, it was his initial calculation that was at fault, not yours. True, there is a danger of pricing yourself out of the market, but any fee should compensate you for the extra work and for the extra risk you are undoubtedly carrying.

Checklist: Partial Services

1 Always have a written agreement defining the limits of your
responsibility.

2 When taking over another party's work, obtain a fee that allows for
familiarisation.

3 When others will be taking over your work, ensure the documentation carries warnings about the extent to which it may be relied upon.

4 If you do not contract for a design liability, ensure that you do not
acquire one inadvertently.

5 If you are employed for 'supervision only', either insist on the architect's normal powers to order opening up or re-building of bad work, or
explain the limits this places on your effectiveness.

6 Particularly when working with in-house architects, insist on the
right to use your own judgement.

7 Never make payment of your fees conditional on obtaining planning
permission.

2.5 Design-build

An area of work in which architects are becoming increasingly involved is
design-build. The expression needs some explanation, particularly for those
readers who thought it to be no more than a euphemism for 'package deal'.
There are, in fact, two entirely different methods of building procurement,
both of which are described as design–build. There are some who might say
there are three: the dedicated design–build organisation; the general contractor who maintains an in-house architect's department; and the general
contractor who employs outside consultants.
At the risk of inflaming opinions, I would suggest that only the first category has
true legitimacy, and so far there are very few firms of any stature in the field.
As a method of building procurement, it has much to commend it, and with
the law of liability as it exists at present, it may present some pointers for the
future. In essence, the system depends on a completely integrated firm controlled by architects and builders equally. Given that it has adequate
insurance arrangements and is itself stable, the firm accepts full responsibility
for the final product to rather more stringent standards than where the
product has been procured by more traditional methods. With buildings
procured in this manner, there is an implied warranty of 'fitness for purpose',
but it is the company that provides the warranty, not the architect personally.
The architects in the company have no contractual duty to the customers or
clients, although they still have the common law duty of care. Similarly, all

members of the company may have a tortious liability to those 'who within their
reasonable contemplation may rely upon their skill and care'. But, as in all
cases of tortious liability, the negligent party has to be clearly identified, and
within a substantial company structure this may not be easy.

One aspect of the design–build organisation that has not, so far as I am aware,
been subjected to any official scrutiny is the conflict that may arise between an
architect's responsibility to his company, and the duty laid on him by the RIBA
Code of Conduct to have regard to the interests 'of those who may use and enjoy
the product of his work'. Certainly, it can be said that where the company is
controlled jointly by architects and builders, the conflict is less likely to arise
than in a general contractor's architect's department.

2.5.1 The in-house architect's department

Where a general contractor maintains an architect's department, he is able to
offer a design–build service as an alternative to the traditional arrangements.
Essentially, the architect's department is a part of the sales promotion of the
contracting side of the organisation, the main attraction to the customer being
an apparent saving of professional fees — and, more particularly, of the VAT
that professional fees carry. Very often, these architect's departments are
presented as something akin to a professional consultancy practice and, with
the recent changes in the RIBA Code of Conduct, there is a real possibility
that this will increasingly be the case.

As a consultant professional myself, I view these arrangements with consideration concern, because of the uncertainty they raise in the customer's (client's)
mind as to the precise nature of the architectural service he is being offered, and
as to the various responsibilities arising from it. I am also extremely concerned
about the personal liability of the professional staffs, who are almost invariably
subordinate to the contracting activities of the company. They have little
control over how they are presented and they may well find themselves with
personal liability in later years. Legally and professionally, they cannot fail to
be more vulnerable than their salaried colleagues in private practice, and I
would refer them to Chapter 3, where the problems are set out in greater detail.

2.5.2 Independent professionals

In-house architect's departments impose on the design/build concept the constraint that the available talent and skill are limited. The system works quite
well where the building project is simple or repetitive, but it has little to offer to
the client with a complex project, or who is looking for specific design talents. It
is, in part, to meet this need that a new concept of design/build has arisen, in
which the contractor assembles the professional team specifically for an
individual project or series of projects. In these cases, the professionals are all
independent consultants but under contract to the builder, who charges on an
inclusive basis for the completed building. How is the architect's liability
affected by this change in the conventional roles? It depends very much on the
written terms of the various agreements, but the most important factor to bear
in mind is that the package carries with it an implied warranty of 'fitness for
purpose'. The architect should guard against taking the burden of that

warranty on his own shoulders. IF he does accept this additional onus, then he should make sure that his insurers know all about it, and accept it — otherwise, if he is sued for breach of that warranty, he may find his insurers walking away from any liability beyond that applicable to lack of skill and care.

The architect should be careful to spell out to his builder client any *professional* responsibility he may feel towards the customer ('those who will use and enjoy'), and it is necessary to define the builder's role in the design process. I raise this matter because one of the most-quoted benefits of design–build is the input at the design stage of the builder's construction expertise. Buildability (and profitability) have inevitable and often far-reaching effects on the design of a building. There the practitioner is in a much stronger position than his salaried in-house colleague, but this serves only to place on him a greater responsibility to use his professional judgement in incorporating the builder's design input.

Often this type of design–build arrangement also implies an element of 'partial service'. There is some justification for this, and the builder may well undertake to obtain or prepare part of the production information. He may also declare that he does not require 'site supervision'. Fair enough, but he will often ask the architect to 'keep an eye on' certain aspects, such as quality or appearance. Just remember that, when you go on site, you acquire a liability to all sorts of people — including the customer. The customer, who is footing the bill, may well insist that the architect performs the normal site inspection functions. Beware! Who are you acting for? Insist that you remain under the contractor's umbrella — you cannot be employed by the builder and undertake a direct responsibility to the customer at the same time. There is a massive conflict of interest, and even declaring it is no answer to the dilemma.

It is worth observing that a builder providing design–build services will often set up a separate company for that precise purpose. There is administrative convenience in this, with the builder's contracting company as a separate entity also being directly employed. The design–build organisation may have a formal contract with the building company, in which case the architect could be employed to perform full site–inspection duties with the same sanctions enjoyed in the conventional arrangement. On the face of it, this might appear an ideal arrangement, but the architect cannot fail to be aware that the two hats surmount the same face. He should not allow his judgement or actions to be impaired by his knowledge.

Finally — until design–build is more commonly used and more widely understood, tell your insurers if you enter into any slightly unusual arrangements. It is better to be safe than sorry.

Checklist: Design-build

1 Ensure that your own position as the *builder's* architect is made clear to the customer.

2 Ensure that the builder understands and acknowledges your responsibilities to the customer — 'those who will use and enjoy . . .'.

3 Avoid assuming any responsibility for 'fitness for purpose'.

4 Avoid 'site supervision' unless you have properly defined and acknowledged power of inspection together with sanctions.

5 Design-build is usually 'fast-track'. Ensure the builder understands the programme implications.

6 Maintain your independent professional judgement at all times.

2.6 Responsibility for consultants

Very few building projects can today be executed without the incursion of one or more (often several more) consultants in various specialisations. Over the years, I have observed with both interest and concern the increasing proliferation of consultants, each of whom has created an institute or association to protect and promote his interests. At least in part, it must be said, the specialists have arisen in response to a growing technological emphasis in the design and equipment of buildings. Also in part, the proliferation is no more than the result of the success of these specialists in promoting legislation in technical terms, the comprehension of which just about validates the degree courses it is now fashionable to undergo. Finally, as a profession, we have brought the situation upon ourselves by permitting and encouraging the usurpation of our roles in all those nitty-gritty areas which are not nearly so satisfying as conceptual design.

I own to expressing a personal bitterness in the above paragraph, but there is no doubt that in some areas our profession has been blinded and rendered impotent by science to an inordinate degree. In large projects, the input of the specialists is clearly an essential and invaluable component of the design process. If only the architect did not so often find himself carrying part or all of the responsibility for it!

Part 2 of the *Architect's appointment* describes 'services which may be provided by the architect to augment the preliminary and basic services described in part 1 or which may be the subject of a separate appointment. The list of services so described is not exhaustive'. The list includes some 44 items of service, many of which fall directly within the architect's remit, but others which will often appropriately fall within the expertise of specialists. The architect will often be taking responsibility for them while actually taking advice from a specialist appointed either directly by the client or sometimes by himself. The *Architect's appointment* then goes on to list under 2.45 the services normally provided by consultants as follows.

'a Quantity surveying
b Structural engineering
c Mechanical engineering
d Electrical engineering
e Landscape and garden design
f Civil engineering
g Town planning
h Furniture design
j Graphic design
k Industrial design
l Interior design'

That list is certainly not exhaustive, because it does not include sanitary engineering, security services and fire safety engineering, space planning (whatever that may be), acoustic design, traffic engineering and highway design, illuminating engineering, and so on.

It is to be hoped that one will never have on any one job the total battery of 15 or 20 specialist consultants, but the probability is that at some time in one's career, each and every one of these, and even more esoteric consultancies, will be required. Few jobs can be run without any consultants at all; in most there are three or four consultants, and six to ten is common. So what does the *Architect's appointment* have to say about the nomination of consultants?

'Consultants may be nominated by either the client or the architect, subject to acceptance by each party.

'Where the client employs the consultants, either directly or through the agency of the architect, the client will hold each consultant, and not the architect, responsible for the competence, general inspection, and performance of the work entrusted to that consultant; provided that in relation to the execution of such work under the contract between the client and the contractor, nothing in this clause shall affect any responsibility of the architect for issuing instructions or for other functions ascribed to the architect under that contract.

'The architect will have the authority to co-ordinate and integrate into the overall design the services provided by any consultant, however employed.'

In part 1 of the document, consultants are referred to all the way through, virtually, each stage stating 'with other consultants where appointed . . .'

2.6.1. *Approving the appointment of consultants*
I have referred elsewhere to the architect's responsibility in the simple act of nominating a consultant, but it is worth raising here the fact that the appointment of any consultant is subject to the acceptance of that consultant either by the employer or by the architect. Quite simply, if you have had a bad experience

with a consultant, then there is no obligation on you to accept him in your project. If you fail to exercise that right and then get into difficulties, you will only have yourself to blame. I appreciate that it is not easy to refuse the appointment of a consultant habitually used by the client, particularly if that consultant is a 'household name'.

It is not always politic to make an issue of such a matter, and in my own practice I have had the galling experience of having to accept a consultant with whom I had previously declared I would never work again. Predictably, we received no better service the second time than on the original occasion. But the principle remains — the architect does have rights in this matter, and he should exercise them if he has any doubts about the competence of a consultant nominated by the client. There is one golden rule, and that is that consultants should always be employed by the client directly. From this it follows that the consultant is paid by the client, is directly responsible to the client, and the client 'will hold each consultant, and not the architect, responsible for the competence, general inspection, and performance of the work entrusted to him'.

Notwithstanding the golden rule, consultants are only too often appointed by the architect, and often paid by him. Sometimes the architect will agree an inclusive fee; on other occasions, the fees will be treated as a disbursement. There are two principal reasons for departing from the golden rule. It may be that the client expresses a desire to have one single bill for professional services, or it may be that the architect wishes to give the impression that he can provide a comprehensive service. In particular, an architect faced with the competitive power of the multi-disciplinary practice often feels himself at a disadvantage when he recommends the appointment of a battery of specialists, and in his keeness to show that he can provide an equivalent service, wittingly and recklessly takes on his own shoulders the whole burden of responsibility to the client for the services of the consultants.

There are ways of at least ameliorating the risks inherent in these procedures, but they do imply openness with the client. I was faced with this problem myself back in the 1960s when, for one client in particular, the same team of architect, quantity surveyor, and structural and M& E engineers was engaged on a series of development contracts. The client was one of those who wanted a single bill for professional fees, and the fee basis was worked out to provide a single percentage, being the aggregate of the four fees involved. It was quite a common procedure, and I held letters of indemnity from the other consultants. When my insurers draw attention to the hazards of this kind of arrangement, I arranged for an exchange of letters between myself and the client, which made it clear that I was appointing the other consultants solely as an agent on behalf of the client, and there was a further exchange of letters between the client and the consultants, creating a direct responsibility in respect of their individual services between the client and each consultant. It can be pointed out to the client with absolute fairness that he is better protected by making this arrangement than by relying solely on the architect and the architect's insurance cover. The fact remains, however, that whatever steps you take to ensure that consultants are directly responsible to clients, whatever indemnities you hold from the consultants, and whatever care you take in correspondence and in your dealings with the consultants, if something goes wrong with a consultant's work, you will not avoid involvement in the subsequent litigation. Just have a look at the following extracts from the description of basic services in the *Architect's appointment*.

1.11   With other consultants where appointed, advise the client of the implications . . .

1.13   With other consultants where appointed, develop the scheme design . . .

1.14   With other consultants where appointed, carry out cost checks . . .

1.16   With other consultants where appointed, prepare production information . . .

1.23   With other consultants where appointed, make where required periodic financial reports . . .

There is almost no aspect of the building contract where the work of the architect and of the consultants is not so inextricably inter–related that a fault can be ascribed only to one party rather than to both or several.

In a case, now happily ruled out of time, in which my own practice was involved, a building erected in the early 1970s suffered from problems with the air-conditioning installation. The consultant had a direct responsibility to the client, but the claims were directed against the consultant, the architect, the builder, the air-conditioning subcontractor, and the supplier of the equipment which was the cause of most of the trouble. As a firm, we were involved in some eight years of legal and technical tussle, with all the attendant time, trouble, and expense. I mention this case, which is typical, to show that there is no way in which the architect can remain free of his responsibility for every aspect of the building in which he is involved. Even if, at the end of the day, he is found not to be liable, he will have had to travel a long, tortuous, and very expensive path in order to clear himself. So it is necessary to be immaculate in one's arrangements with consultants and in one's dealings with them.

2.6.2 Dealing with consultants

I referred earlier to the obtaining of indemnities from consultants. It is a reasonable precaution, if only to remind the consultant of his responsibilities. But its value is only as great as the financial resource of the consultant himself, and it depends on his maintaining his own insurance arrangements in an adequate sum and dealing with his insurers in accordance with the terms of his policy. This is something over which the architect has absolutely no control. In the case I have referred to, the consultant was insured for a sum which was a mere fraction of the value of the claim, and he failed to inform his insurers when he should have done that there was a likelihood of a claim arising. He was extremely fortunate that the insurers stood behind him during the eight-year battle.

There is an understandable tendency among architects to develop close and informal arrangements with consultants, particularly when they habitually work with them. It may be tedious and present a real problem with paper storage, but you cannot be too punctilious in recording properly all your dealings with consultants. If you make a decision based on the advice of a consultant, then it should be clearly recorded in a minute or letter to him. It is very difficult, after the passage of years, to establish which decisions were made on the advice of, and with the knowledge of, the consultant and which were the product of the architect's own fertile imagination. Only recently, I was asked to sign an architect's instruction confirming alterations that had taken place to some reinforcement in the foundations of a building. A change which was comparatively minor (I think) had been instructed by the engineer in the course of a site visit, and it had actually been carried out by the time I issued the instruction for it to be done. According to any book, this must be bad practice, but it is the sort of thing that happens on most sites if work is to proceed in anything like an expeditious manner. But the engineer's instruction had been verbal, and we had not a single scrap of evidence in the office that it was an engineer's decision and not ours. This is what goes on with every job and with virtually every consultant. We couldn't build in any other way. But how many consultants take a triplicate pad on site with them to record all these minor decisions, with a copy to the architect so that he knows just what is going on? Too few, I fear.

Perhaps the greatest burden the architect has to bear in relation to consultants is the 'co-ordination of their work'. Many of the problems arise from the fact that consultants tend to work in a different way from architects, apart from relying on subcontractors and suppliers to do much of the detailing for them far into the contract period. This is particularly so with mechanical and electrical services, but it applies to other specialisms also. This circumstance leads, very often, to ad-hoc changes to other work while it is actually proceeding on site, and ad-hoc decisions often start off a chain reaction, the result of which is difficult to predict. This is a problem that only the various institutes can sort out between themselves, and a major study of this topic is proceeding at the present time. I hold out no great hopes for a solution in the near future, and the architect will continue to carry the can, at least in part, for those elements of a building which are primarily the product and the responsibility of other professions.

2.6.3 The BPF system

A recent development in this area is the publication by the British Property Federation of their system for the design and construction of buildings. Within their system, the design leader (who should in most cases be an architect) has to accept responsibility for the whole of the pre-tender design. It is too early to judge whether the system will be widely adopted, but if you are involved with the system as 'design leader', then the above advice cannot apply. In the RIBA's initial response to the BPF, it was stated that if the client required this kind of single and total responsibility, then the design leader must be permitted to employ all the sub-consultants directly, on terms decided by the design leader. The design leader should have complete authority, including rights of dismissal. While this may not do much to reduce the design leader's responsibility, it does at least place him in control of as much of the situation as possible. In any event, if you are appointed design leader in this way, then inform your insurers.

Checklist: Consultants

1 Consultants should always be appointed by, and responsible to, the client.

2 If the architect appoints, he should do so as the 'client's agent'.

3 Ensure that a consultant's appointment is compatible with the service you require from him.

4 Never pass instructions on consultants' work without evidence in writing of the consultants' intention.

5 If you have reason to suspect the competence of a proposed consultant, you have the right to object to his appointment. Do so.

6 If you appoint consultants yourself, inform your insurers when you do so.

3: MINIMISING THE IMPACT

3.1 The certainty of claims

The first part of this book has been devoted to explaining how the law of liability operates, and how in the pursuit of his professional activities the architect can place himself at risk or, by the proper arrangement of his work, reduce that risk to a minimum.

It must be quite clear, however, that with the risks inherent in the building process, there will be times when, even with the greatest care and the best management in the world, a building failure will occur, and no architect engaged in the construction process can ever be free from the possibility of a claim.

In reading the preceding chapters, you may have come to the conclusion that, if you follow all the advice that is given, you will merely have substituted the frying pan of liability for the fire of bankruptcy. I will not harp on the inadequacies of the architect's remuneration, but just as the architect is for ever balancing the conflicting requirements in his buildings, so he has to balance his risk of claims against his ability to survive in a harsh economic world.

Counsels of perfection are all very well, but corners will inevitably be cut in some places, and there will be times when there will be delegation without proper supervision. The risks inherent in these decisions have to be accepted if we are to survive at all.

Over and above that, even the most immaculate procedures will not protect you against the deliberately malicious client, the crook, the twister, and the rogue.

In the last five years, one in five of the smallest practices received either threats of action or actual writs, and this percentage rises rapidly with practice size: one third of all three- to five-man practices have been similarly treated, and two thirds of all practices with six to 10 personnel. In practices above 10 technical personnel, there is virtually none which within the past five years has not been in receipt of claims. It is even more worrying that over the five-year period, the rate at which claims are being reported has more that doubled, and one does not need to be a mathematician or clairvoyant to predict that, in a lifetime of architectural practice, literally nobody is safe from the fear of claims.

So, accepting the inevitability that claims will arise, the second part of this book deals with the ways open to an architect of avoiding the event of a claim turning into a cataclysm of personal disaster.

Some of the expedients dealt with below do not enjoy my personal approval: they are included because they are available and, to the best of my knowledge, do not infringe the RIBA's Code of Conduct. In a sense, their inclusion for serious consideration is a commentary on the iniquity of the burden of liability carried by architects. If they were adopted widely, I believe that architecture as a profession, enjoying public repute and respect, would cease to be.

There are many roads to relative safety. The choice of which ones to take is yours.

Out of the frying pan

3.2 Suitable and adequate insurance

No aspect of liability can be discussed without also considering the question of insurance. There are those who believe that many of our liability problems stem directly from the growth of indemnity insurance. Certainly, there is anecdotal evidence of clients who, having established that there is adequate insurance, have deliberately embarked on a course towards a claim. Certainly, the knowledge that insurance exists helps to salve the conscience of a client contemplating a claim: 'Well, old boy, the insurance will pay. I'm not getting at you personally'. And many are the clients who would stay their hand if they thought that their claim would jeopardise the livelihood and savings of their architect.

Having said that, and while deploring the evil side-effects of insurance, it is my personal belief that no responsible professional practitioner, unless he is possessed of very substantial means (which he is prepared to place at risk), can afford to be without suitable and adequate insurance cover.

Let us face it, none of us is infallible: with the best will and greatest care in the world, accidents can happen. Even the best architects are liable at some time to drop a great and irretrievable clanger. First and foremost, insurance cover exists to provide the means to make good the situation, so that the client will not suffer as a result of his trusted adviser's defect. And who would want it otherwise?

This section is titled 'Suitable and adequate insurance', a short phrase that embraces a number of extremely complex matters. Next to staff salaries and rent, professional indemnity insurance is probably the largest single outgoing of an architectural practice. Not only is it a major expense, it may be all that stands between an architect and bankruptcy and total financial and professional disaster. So it is worth spending a considerable amount of thought on getting your insurance provisions right. I will deal elsewhere with the parallel routes by which you can seek to protect your private position. But none of the protection you may be able to organise is completely certain — insurance is the great safety-net for your client and yourself.

Given the expense and importance of your professional indemnity insurance, it is only good sense to make sure that what you are buying is what you actually want — and that what you want is truly going to serve your needs. Like that of most of the population, my view of insurance tends to be rather cynical and is encapsulated in the definition, 'Comprehensive insurance provides cover for everything except that which actually occurs'. Perhaps this is better expressed by the injunction always to read the small print.

Although the fashion for printing insurance policies in four-point diamond type is no longer in, nonetheless any policy is a long and complicated document. A chore and a bore it may be — but read it, understand it, and if it does not suit your particular circumstances, negotiate for an endorsement that does.

3.2.1 The basis of PI insurance

When you buy professional indemnity insurance, you become a party to a contract. It is as well to know something about the history and basis of that contract.

First, it is a contract of indemnity. In return for your premium, the insurers

'Nothing personal!'

undertake to indemnify you against your losses arising from certain stated causes up to the limits laid down in the policy.

Indemnity means that they will reimburse you the actual loss you have incurred. While policies vary in their actual wording, the 'loss' in professional indemnity policies is usually defined as monies which you are *legally obliged to pay* as a result of some negligent act or omission in the performance of your professional activities. The legal obligation to pay is very important and may have some strange side-effects. If, for instance, in the middle of a job you discover a palpable error, the insurers will not reimburse you with the cost of paying the builder to put it right. Now it may be possible to negotiate something with your insurers, but if they won't play ball, you may be in a difficulty. Professionally, you have to do something about the error — but do not confess your error to your client before you have notified your insurers and taken their instructions.

There will be a limit of indemnity — after all, the insurers will want to know just what they are in for. Until quite recently, most indemnity policies were written with what is known as an 'aggregate indemnity'. Under such a policy, you could have any number of claims — but the liability of the insurers was limited to the aggregate sum. If the selected aggregate was inadequate to settle all the claims in full, the architect would be reimbursed as each claim was settled or adjudicated — and thenceforth would be on his own. Today, it is increasingly common for policies to be written on an 'each and every claim' basis. In a sense, this means that the underwriters' exposure is completely unlimited, because they have no way of knowing in advance how many claims may be made during the currency of the policy. Because their risk is so much greater, insurers are (rightly) increasingly sensitive to the quality of the information on which they base their premiums.

Perhaps most importantly, professional indemnity insurance is an annual contract. It covers the insured in respect of those matters which are notified to the underwriters during the currency of the policy. The event giving rise to the claim could have occurred 10, 20, 30 or more years previously, and settlement may be one, five, or ten years hence. This aspect of insurance is probably the greatest single cause of misunderstanding, and it is well worth more than a passing thought. It is dealt with more fully in the sections on the proposal form and notification.

3.2.2 Utmost good faith
Some years ago, I wrote in an article that insurance was the only contract based on the mutual distrust of the parties. While that may be so in reality, the law takes a different view. As is usual, it is phrased in Latin: *uberrima fide* — utmost good faith. The significance of this is that the insurance is initiated by the insured through the medium of the proposal form — that is where the utmost good faith has its origin. That is where most allegations of bad faith by the insurers originate. Your proposal form is all the insurer has to guide him when he assesses the premium he wishes to charge — or even whether to accept the risk at all. For your insurance to be proof against repudiation or avoidance, the proposal form must disclose all relevant facts of which you are or should be

aware which could have a bearing on the underwriters' assessment of the risk. It may not be sufficient simply to answer the questions on the form if you are aware of some factor not covered by the questions which could be significant. Nor is it sufficient to answer briefly or ambiguously if a longer, clearer answer would put the insurers on guard.

However, insurers do not have it all their own way. Because the policy document is produced by the insurers, the law has it that any ambiguity or uncertainties in that document shall be construed in favour of the insured. Also, insurers may not repudiate liability or void a policy simply because of an error or omission in the proposal form. The defect has to be of a nature that would have affected their consideration of the risk.

3.2.3 The QC clause

Because the insurers have to pick up the tab at the end of the day, in virtually all policies they claim the right if they wish to take over the defence of any claim. They may decide to fight, or they may wish to settle, and you might consider either course against your best interests. Such a conflict of interest, and it is by no means uncommon, is usually resolved through the medium of what in most policies is called the 'QC clause'. If the QC clause is invoked, then the dispute between underwriters and insured is put to independent leading counsel for an opinion. If he says there is a good defence, then the architect has either to allow the defence to proceed, or to make his own settlement without the benefit of his indemnity. It can, of course, go the other way, and the insurers may be forced to continue with very expensive litigation on a monetarily small matter of principle that they would have been happy to settle in order to be rid of it.

3.2.4 What sum to cover

Given the basic necessity of insurance, practitioners are faced with the almost impossible task of deciding the amount for which they should insure. One simple approach is to buy cover for the largest sum you can afford. It may still be insufficient, but seldom will it be too great. It is always worthwhile seeking quotes for various levels of cover, and you may be pleasantly surprised to find how little the higher levels of cover cost. Although it is the multi-million pound claims that hit the headlines, numerically by far the majority of claims are for comparatively modest sums, and it is the lowest level of cover that is the most expensive.

There are various rules of thumb that can be applied, the most common being a multiplier of the annual fee-turnover. A commonly recommended figure is three times turnover, and this is being quoted as the qualifying minimum in a scheme for group top-up insurance now under discussion. Any mutiplier should be subject to a minimum figure, the most commonly quoted being £250,000. At the upper end of the scale, rules of thumb do not work, and the large firm has to make an informed judgement on the basis of historical record and a true assessment of the risk.

Against this, public clients have recently established a general rule to require private consultants to insure for a minimum of £250,000 or twice annual fee turnover, and the information from the RIBA's liability survey confirms that as generally adequate protection for clients.

Only a few years ago, the largest claim sustained against a firm of architects was little over £½m. Today, multi-million pound claims are comparatively common-place, although it is doubtful whether cover above £5m is necessary for any firm of architects, at the time of writing.

For the new practitioner, particularly one engaged on small works with no tail of work behind him, minimum insurance may be all that is required. But claims have a habit of dragging on, and the effect of inflation can be dramatic. Minimum cover that looked adequate when a claim was notified can have a very different appearance five years later. Until recently, my own policy had an open claim against it which was notified in 1976. Before it was struck out, the lawyers estimated that it might have come to trial in 1985/86. As it happens, our liability in that case was very small or non-existent — but had our cover been only just adequate in 1976, we would have a very large uninsured loss in 1986 if the courts had found against us. You may think that you would not let one of your cases drag on for 10 years — that you would settle. Unfortunately, you may have no control in the matter and no redress against the delaying parties.

So in looking at the adequacy of your cover, you need both hindsight and fore-sight. Look at the size and length of your tail, and project any anticipated liability forward at least five years. Difficult? Yes, but very necessary. If there is a grain of comfort in this situation, it is that claimants seldom pursue practitioners into bankruptcy. If they can see that you have insured responsi-bly (although, in the event, inadequately), they will usually settle for what they can get from the insurers, with perhaps a token personal payment.

3.2.5 *What is covered*

Most policies provide that the stated indemnity limit shall be in respect of moneys you may be legally obliged to pay in respect of the claim. This covers not only damages that may be awarded against you, but also the legal costs of the claimant. The costs incurred in the defence of a claim are usually borne by your insurers themselves, although this is not invariably so, and particularly with some of the low-premium policies, the indemnity limit has to cover the defence costs as well. In the case of the major insurers, the only time you will have to bear any of the defence costs yourself is if the total adjudication against you exceeds your indemnity limit. If, for instance, you are insured for £¼m and the claimant is awarded £200,000 plus £100,000 costs, then you will have to find one-sixth of the defence costs out of your own pocket, as well as the £50,000 shortfall on the general indemnity. So in assessing the level of indemnity you wish to purchase, always take into account the question of the other side's costs, which could quite easily amount to 50 per cent of the value of the damages, and maybe more.

Your policy will not normally cover you for your own direct costs in defending a claim. These can be a matter of no small consequence, and there is little you can do about it. If you do receive a claim, you are going to be involved in time and expense in searching files, reproducing documents and drawings, attending conferences, making statements, and so on. For the small practitioner, this can be particularly onerous and may even lead to neglect of current work, exposing him to future claims as a result. This is just one of the more unfortunate side-effects of a negligence claim. Enquiries I have made about the possibility of extending the standard insurance to cover defence costs have proved fruitless. But it was indicated to me that, if a market could be established, it would result in premiums increasing by 25 to 33 per cent. That in itself is an indication of the size of the uncovered burden.

3.2.6 Whom to insure with

Having decided on the amount of your cover, what sort of insurance should you buy — and from whom? About 65 per cent of practices currently arrange their indemnity insurance through the ABS Insurance Agency Ltd, who negotiate a standard policy with a single company. Another 15 per cent go through APIA (Architects & Professional Indemnity Agency), who place the insurance in the Lloyds market. Other policies are available both through companies and at Lloyds, most concentrating on the lower levels of cover or special cases — particularly those with bad claims records, consortium arrangements, and the like.

The most important point to consider in deciding on your insurers is continuity. You will, hopefully, be in practice a long time, and there is no greater hazard to face than discontinuous cover. Remember, your insurance is an annual contract, and the problems that arise if your insurers decide to withdraw from the market can be traumatic. (These problems are dealt with in detail below.) So insist on using insurers with a long record in the field.*

The choice between a company policy and Lloyds cover is more difficult to make, although the Lloyds back-up in the event of syndicate failure may be marginally safer than the compensation funds organised by the companies. Incidentally, it is worth noting that Lloyds cover may embrace companies as underwriters — but the companies are then considered as ordinary Lloyds members.

3.2.7 What sort of cover

There are two basic kinds of cover you can purchase: 'each and every claim', or aggregate. It is generally recommended that you opt for the first, because in our profession lightning can regrettably strike twice in the same year. In fact, if you think about the way architects work, the odds on there being more than one claim in a year are quite substantial. We tend to work in phases, using the same details in a number of jobs, or even doing a number of similar jobs simul-taneously or in succession. So if there is one failure, there is quite likely to be another.

If you have insured for a sum you think will cover the worst failure that is likely to happen, but have insured in aggregate, one claim may exhaust your cover, leaving you exposed if you have more than one claim in the policy year. With 'each and every claim' cover, this cannot happen. If you do insure in aggregate, then you probably need a much higher figure.

---

* *This was written before the New Hampshire Insurance Company, insuring 65 per cent of the profession, decided to withdraw. Even a long history is no guarantee of future performance.*

3.2.8 What size excess

Your insurers will always require that you bear the first stated amount of any claim. That figure may range from a few hundred to several thousand pounds, depending on the extent of your cover.

If you volunteer to bear an increased excess, this will be reflected in a reduced premium. Alternatively, for the same premium you may be able to purchase considerably higher cover. If you view your insurance as a safeguard against disaster, this is well worth consideration. But be careful — the excess is payable on each and every claim, and a run of quite small claims could be a real embarrassment.

This is particularly true if you are engaged on estate housing, and it is as well to check carefully your policy wording. Some policies state that the excess is payable on *every claim*. Others require the excess to be payable only once where a succession of claims arises from the same negligent act. A single incorrect detail built into 50 houses can give rise to 50 separate claims, and to be liable for 50 excesses could wipe out even a well-established firm.

In most policies, the excess is payable only if the insurers have to actually pay out on a claim. There are some policies in which the wording is rather different, and even where a notification is settled without a formal claim being made or a settlement being agreed, the defence and investigation costs incurred by the insurers are a first charge on the excess. This needs to be watched very carefully, because claims arise only out of about one notification in three, and not all claims end with a settlement, so you could finish up having paid out several excesses, even though no money has actually been paid out to claimants.

3.2.9 Additional cover

With the essentials of your insurance decided, there are a number of extensions to the policy that are commonly available. Whether you adopt them is a matter of individual choice and will depend on your type of practice, your clientele, and so on. The following notes will help you to a decision. Additional covers are usually provided either as an option or as standard, but with a much lower limit of indemnity. Where the additional cover is standard for no additional premium, the limit of this extended cover will usually be 10 per cent of the prime indemnity limit or £25,000, whichever is lower. Higher cover is generally available for an additional premium.

3.2.9.1. Libel and slander

The cover is only for damages incurred as a consequence of your professional practice. You (and I) are not covered for anything published in the media. You are also not covered for your costs in prosecuting a libel or slander suit against anybody else.

3.2.9.2 Infringement of copyright

Cover is for your costs in prosecuting a claim against somebody else for breach of your copyright. If you are sued for breaching somebody else's copyright, you may be on your own. Architects today are increasingly engaged on the refurbishment and extension of other architect's buildings. It is very easy inadvertently to breach another designer's copyright. The leading case is the Heal's furniture store in London, where the widow of the original architect sued for breach of copyright when the building was extended to the original design. Nowadays, that situation is normally covered in the terms relating to copyright in the Terms of Engagement or *Architect's appointment* — but you cannot be sure, so it may be worth extending your policy to cover this risk.

3.2.9.3 Additional legal representation

This will cover the cost of legal representation of yourself at a court or tribunal of enquiry if the underwriters think you should be represented to protect your (and their) interests under the other sections of the policy.

The extension does not cover your representation in the criminal courts or at any disciplinary enquiry by, for instance, the RIBA or ARCUK.

It also does not cover any penalty or costs awarded against you (although they may be covered by the main indemnity).

3.2.9.4 Fee recovery

This is an optional extension and is usually much hedged in by conditions. Your insurers are not debt collectors, nor are they a trade indemnity organisation. The main point to bear in mind is that the non-payment of fees is usually because the client is short of money, or he is dissatisfied with his architect, or he is not a very nice person. Therefore, pressure on the client to pay up may predictably precipitate a negligence claim against you, justified or not. I suspect that the protection afforded by this part of the insurance cover may be illusory — particularly as it does not cover you for any costs awarded against you if you lose, and is anyway subject to excess. Read the conditions very carefully and then make up your own mind.

3.2.9.5 Loss of documents

Whether you insure under your professional indemnity policy or through your office contents policy, you certainly need cover for loss of documents. This is not just in case you leave your briefcase in a taxi, but because your office may go up in flames. There are two separate kinds of costs which may be incurred as a result of such a disaster, and they are both difficult to predict: replacement of the lost documents, and consequential losses to third parties to whom you owe a duty.

If you do have a burn-out, you are not going to be able to replace all the lost papers, nor, in all probability, will you wish to. Much of the mountain of paper in any architect's office is of only ephemeral use and interest. If your archives are on paper, you may regret not having microfilmed them, but there is little you can do in practice.

But what about current jobs — the drawings, correspondence, approvals, contracts, subcontracts, and the rest? Fortunately, the bulk of them will exist in original or copy somewhere else and, if you have not made yourself too unpopular, most people or firms will be fairly co-operative about letting you have copies. There will be a hefty commitment of time and copying costs if you have to recreate negatives, and this needs to be considered.

Actual re-drawing cost will probably be limited to the work carried out in the office in the previous few weeks, and hopefully you will be able to do these drawings rather more quickly the second time around.

That more or less covers the physical cost of document replacement. But what about the consequential losses? You will have contracts with clients, who in turn will have contracts with builders and others. Failure to provide drawings when a builder requires them may involve your client in payments for delays on the contract and perhaps losses in other directions. There are many ways in which your misfortune may be visited upon others and may sometimes finish up as an additional charge on yourself.

While I have no knowledge of a client compounding the problems of a burnt-out architect by suing for his consequential loss, it is a hard world we live in, and your client may be no better placed to sustain the loss than you are yourself. If you are going to insure against loss of documents, try to ensure that consequential losses are also covered.

Checklist: Suitable and adequate insurance

1 Make sure the cover you buy truly serves your purpose. Unsuitable cover may be no better than none.

2 The professional indemnity policy is an annual contract.

3 It is a policy of indemnity and covers what you may be legally obliged to pay.

4 The limit of indemnity will have to cover costs awarded against you. With some policies, it also has to cover defence costs.

5 The limit of indemnity should preferably be in respect of 'each and every claim'.

6 Utmost good faith requires that you disclose all relevant information (of which you may be aware) in the proposal form.

7 Insist on a QC clause to protect your right to settle or defend, against the wishes of the insurers.

8 The recommended minimum level of cover is the greater of £250,000 or three times average fee income, but you should always try to make a realistic appraisal of the risk — allowing for inflation!

9 Accepting a higher excess can reduce premium or purchase higher cover — but beware of multiple claims.

3.3 The insurance proposal form

Insurance contracts are based on the concept of 'utmost good faith'. Whether you believe that they are always operated that way is neither here nor there. Discovery that you have not completed the proposal form in utmost good faith may well invalidate your insurance just when you need it most. The concept is unarguable: the insurer or underwriter quotes a premium on the basis of what you tell him. If you tell him less than the whole truth, either deliberately or recklessly, you mislead him into quoting the wrong premium. It is rather akin to backing an outsider and then switching it for a 'ringer'. Insurers do not like that kind of treatment any more than bookies.

So filling in your professional indemnity proposal is an act of some moment, worth spending time over to get it right. If you are a partnership, the completed form should be discussed with all your partners before being signed and despatched. They are all intimately and vitally concerned, particularly the most junior partner who just happens to be possessed of a substantial private fortune! The following questions appear on all the most common forms, not necessarily in this order.

3.2.1 Title of practice (including any former practices for which cover is required)

Your situation may be absolutely simple and straightforward requiring an answer no more complicated than '*Vitruvius*, architect'. But if you are a partnership, and particularly if you have any complicated form of partnership structure, make sure you include all the practice names, including for good measure any service company.

'Former practices' include the former practices of any of the partners who may have practised either individually or in other partnerships before they became partners in the present practice.

It is usual when leaving a practice to obtain an indemnity from the partners you leave behind in respect of your liability for work in that practice. If the firm you are leaving is well established and substantial, then you may feel that the indemnity is all you need. Furthermore, most policies cover 'all existing and past partners' of a practice. However, circumstances do change over the years, and if the previous firm does not maintain adequate cover, or goes out of practice altogether, that indemnity or cover may be worth rather less than the paper it is written on.

By a similar token, if you have left a sole principal, he may die, emigrate, or go bust, and then a prospective claimant will look for the next man in line, who may be one of your partners. So don't take chances: declare the whole of the risk you wish to cover. If the risk is slight, then that will be reflected in the premium, but if the risk is real and substantial, then it must be in your interest to have it covered no matter what the premium is.

3.3.2 Profession(s)/business(es) of practice

Another deceptively simple question. Certainly, if you complete it simply 'architects', this will cover all the activities commonly and usually carried out by architects. This will also include those activities more commonly within the province of other professions, provided they do not assume the proportions of a separate speciality. The big areas of risk are structural engineering, M&E services, and quantity surveying. If you carry out any of these and other specialised activities more than incidentally to your architectural work, then declare it.

With many architects playing around with computers and developing software, a whole new area of risk has opened up. There are two aspects of computer work and they need to be dealt with separately.

The first consists of providing services to other architects on your own computer, using your own or commercial software. Declare the activity. You should have little difficulty obtaining cover, although you may have to pay an additional premium.

The second consists of creating and selling architectural software to other architects. This is not an activity which is normally covered under a professional indemnity policy. It opens up whole new areas of risk and should be separately discussed with your brokers or insurers. It should also be discussed with your lawyers to settle matters of copyright, disclaimers, and so on.

3.3.3 Practice dates
Date of commencement of present practice and date of cessation of previous practices. Ensure that you include even that part-time work you did before you established your first formal practice.

3.3.4 Address or addresses of practice, with the partner or principal responsible for the work at each office
Here we are back to utmost good faith. Many branch offices of largish firms are under the day-to-day control of salaried architects or associates. Provided the person in control is a registered architect, the requirements of the Code of Conduct are met — but is this good enough for your insurers? If the named partner is only nominally in charge, popping in for half a day every week or so, think twice before you put his name on the form without any further explanation. If you have good reason for your implicit faith in the salaried assistant or associate, your insurers will probably agree with you — but at least give them the opportunity to demur.

3.3.5 Names in full of all partners/principals/owners
Straightforward enough if you are a partnership, as all names are on the notepaper. But it is worth a little more thought if you practise in company structure and possibly have outside shareholders. The recent changes in the Code of Conduct have opened up whole new genera of practising arrangements, including limited and unlimited companies, and co-operatives with pretty free-wheeling structures. Make sure that your insurers know just who they are covering, and in case of doubt, attach an explanatory letter, or even a copy of your articles of agreement.

3.3.6 Total numbers of staff
For most firms, this will present no difficulty, but what if you 'employ' contract staff or 'self-employed' personnel or have 'ghosting' arrangements? The

best advice is to declare the exact circumstances, and make sure that, if your arrangements require it, you obtain a waiver of subrogation against these quasi-employees. In fact, the categories of staff set out on standard proposal forms may not fit your actual personnel in a number of ways. Their origins are lost in the murk of history and tradition and bear little relationship to the skills, qualifications, and working arrangements in most modern practices.

3.3.7 *Gross fees for past five years*

These are usually required to be your audited account figures, but if audited accounts are not available, then use the best figures you have. Be prepared to substantiate later whatever figures you use.

Your turnover figure has a large effect on the amount of your premium, so the more accurate the figures are, the better. Guessing at figures high enough to cover will cost you money.

You will note that the form provides columns for splitting your fees into UK and overseas contracts. Different rules are involved when you work outside the UK, both in terms of contract arrangements and the law that might prevail. Similar questions elicit information about building values certified. I always find this question a little naive and wonder how insurers apply it. Much work that an architect does may not end up with certification, so just what significance insurers attach to this answer is probably known only to the insurers.

Insurers require the split of your *gross* fees. Provided you keep reasonable records, you should be able to answer this with a degree of accuracy. A list of various activities is given, with a space for specifying any not on the list.

The last question on the list relates to fees paid by you to independent specialist consultants. This is a very important factor in assessing the risk, and you should be careful to get the answer right. Relationships with consultants have been dealt with above, but what insurers are concerned with here is the extent to which you employ consultants directly, charging a blanket fee to the client and then paying the consultant out of the gross fee. Where the consultant holds a direct appointment from the client and you merely pay his fees as a disbursement, you need not include the figures.

Finally, there is a question regarding your estimated gross fees for the current financial year. While this is only an estimate, you should endeavour to be as accurate as possible. Constant underestimating will show up eventually in the five-year record, and insurers will probably begin to make their own premium adjustment to cover it.

3.3.8 *The type of work you do*

The intent of this question is clear enough in that insurers are trying to get a picture of your workload. What is not so clear is the basis on which insurers want it answered — fees earned, value certified, work resource employed, or a combination of all three. With differing time and fee-scales for different categories of work, this can be a tricky calculation; and if your workload is complicated, it may be worthwhile discussing the matter with your broker or agent and then explaining more fully in an attached letter.

3.3.9 Largest recent contracts
Probably the most straightforward question on the form, but it does presume that the architect is providing full service. To be safe (and honest), you should include any large development where you are providing only partial services.

3.3.10 Overseas work
Insurers are nervous about overseas work, and affirmative answers to these questions will almost certainly precipitate further questions from underwriters. They may well decline to cover certain overseas work under your general policy. Practices contemplating overseas work, whether or not the professional activities are carried out in the UK, should always clear the insurance angle at the outset. Don't undertake the commission and then tell your insurers. The risks are greater and different, and it is quite possible that insurers may lay down conditions that will completely alter your projected costings on the project. Especially in respect of work carried out in the United States, they may decline to cover you at all.

3.3.11 Consortia, group practice, and joint ventures
Your proposal form will have a very full question on this type of endeavour. Read it carefully and answer openly. There is an almost limitless permutation of arrangements between firms and individuals for providing professional services, and unless the arrangements are very carefully documented, with safeguards built in, one party or another could well find himself carrying liabilities that he (and his insurers) had never contemplated.

Your insurers will want to see this documentation, and they are quite likely to propose alterations or safeguards as a pre-condition to cover. If they do, you will be wise to comply. In protecting their interest, the insurers will at the same time be protecting your own. Many consortia and joint ventures come together as a result of some particular project, and getting the project moving usually takes precedence over the formal arrangements. Take time out to get it right and you may save yourself many sleepless nights in the years to come.

An alternative open to you is to take out completely separate cover in respect of consortium work. This may be in the form of either a single–project insurance, or a PI policy covering the entire consortium for all of its work. This is something that should be discussed and agreed with the other members of the consortium. Preferably, the insurance arrangements should be spelt out in the consortium agreement, with cross-indemnities clearly laid down. This is a task for a specialist lawyer. Make sure you provide for what happens when the consortium ceases to exist.

3.3.12 Employment of specialist consultants
The wording of this question shows that insurers recognise the liability problems that may arise from the direct employment of consultants by architects. The RIBA has long recommended that architects should not employ consultants directly, but should ensure that the appointments are made by the client. Unfortunately where the institute proposes, only too often the client disposes.

To many clients, the ideal professional team is one man, and the ideal professional fee is one bill. With a project in the balance, there is strong pressure and temptation to fall in with the client's wishes, but beware. Although insurers are prepared to accept these arrangements, subject to evidence of the consultant's insurance, you may be at greater risk than you realise. You have no guarantee that the consultant will maintain his insurance, or even remain in the country. If a claim arises, it will be directed first at yourself, and your insurers' rights of subrogation may be worth nothing to them. This is the reason for the question on fees. Insurers recognise the greater risk, and it will be reflected in your premiums. So however you answer this question, your general practice should be to press for direct appointment.

Perhaps an acceptable departure from this rule is the sundry bits of advice that all architects habitually seek from friendly consultants. Tell your insurers how you operate, keep it small, and you will probably be all right.

3.3.13 Details of your existing insurance
Straightforward enough, and if you are simply renewing your existing policy, this will present no difficulty. If you are switching to new insurers, then it is very important to make as full a disclosure as you can of your existing arrangements.

3.3.14 Previous insurance proposals
Standard questions regarding previous refusal of cover, quotation of special terms, or cancellations of previous insurance.

Note that the question applies not only to the practice but to all individual partners or principals. So check, particularly with your newest and youngest partner. Do not take it for granted that he is in the clear. You may find that you should have asked the questions before he became a partner.

If you should be tempted to 'forget' a previous refusal of cover or a special loading, remember that the indemnity insurance market is a very small world, and however much insurers may compete with each other for business, they are close-knit in defence of their common interests.

An aspect of this question that I view with some amusement is that relating to special terms or loadings. In truth, as there is no tariff, then there is no such thing as 'special terms'. Or if there is, then most architects are blissfully unaware that they are being quoted to them. The liability survey by the RIBA elicited two highly contradictory facts: that firms without claims paid a much lower premium than firms with claims; and that the vast majority of architects with a claims record averred that it had had no effect on their premiums. The reason for this corporate ignorance is simply the secrecy that shrouds the PI insurance operation. The customer has no yardstick against which to measure his premium.

3.3.15 Amount of cover
This has been fully dealt with above, but remember to state if the sum is required in aggregate or for each and every claim.

3.3.16 Fee recovery extension
See p. 110.

3.3.17 Loss of documents
See pp. 110–11.

3.3.18 Previous claims record
The form will ask for details on all claims (successful or not) made in the past 10
years against the practice or its present and/or past partners. That is a pretty
comprehensive list, but observe that it asks only about claims. It doesn't ask in
this question about all those precautionary notifications you may have made.
If you have been continuously insured with the same insurers over the years,
then they will of course already have your claims record, and it is probably
sufficient to refer to it in those terms. However, if you are seeking competitive
quotes from new insurers, then answering this question fully and accurately is
absolutely crucial.

3.3.19 Circumstances which might give rise to a claim
Many insurers specifically preface their question with: 'Are the partners *after
enquiry*, aware of any circumstances . . .' So in my practice we always make the
enquiry. We do it by circulating a memo throughout the office for signature by
every member of the staff, and we attach that form to our proposal. This is
probably the best you can do: if somebody in the firm is hiding some knowledge of a problem, there is little you can do about it until the chicken comes
home to roost. I deal with the pitfalls of non-disclosure on pp. 121–123.
Sufficient to say here that if you are aware of any upcoming problem, you
should disclose it.
More particularly if you are switching insurers, make sure you do not miss anything out. If you have previously notified a claim to the company that you are
leaving, check that you are covered by all your notifications to them should a
claim actually materialise. It may depend on the wording of your policy, so
don't just assume that because you have notified them, they will pick up the tab
after you have left them.

3.3.20 The declaration
And finally — the declaration. It is salutary to read it aloud at a partners' meeting — or to yourself as a sole principal — before you sign it. Note particularly
that there is an undertaking to inform the insurers if anything changes before
completion of the contract of insurance. So if you sign and despatch the form on
Friday and a threatening letter arrives on the following Monday, do not breathe
a sigh of relief and congratulate yourself on your good luck or foresight in
sending off the form when you did — inform them.
The completion of a PI proposal form is so important that I do not attempt to
summarise the advice I have given. Read it, learn it, and when you have to
complete a proposal form, read it again.

3.4 Dealing with insurers
Professional indemnity insurance is no different from any other insurance, in
that the interests of the insurer and the insured are diametrically opposed.
Insurers are in business to make profits, while the insured seeks to remain in
business at the expense of his insurers. Every time an insured architect advises

his insurers of 'circumstances', or a threat of a claim, or an actual claim, the insurers see a possible loss on their underwriting account in place of their potential profit. Within the fairly strict rules of the game, they will seek to minimise their loss.

This statement of the reality of the insurance contract is made without malice and to set the context within which dealings with the insurers should be conducted. While repudiation of liability is by no means unheard of, it is not the commonest way in which insurers may seek to limit their loss at the expense (not necessarily financial) of the insured.

An understanding of the way insurers work is helpful in getting the best value from your cover and avoiding a lot of heartache and worse. There are people with a greater measure of this understanding than most architects, and if you do have a claim, it is best to take advice from them. If you have placed your insurance through a broker, this is the time to help him earn his not insubstantial commission. Alternatively, you can discuss the problem with your solicitor and have him retain a watching brief on your interests. You will have to pay him yourself, but it is as well to have somebody without a financial interest in the case to advise you. It is with some regret that I do not regard the main professional indemnity broking agencies as the best source of independent advice. Although they are independent of the underwriting operation, they have in their everyday operations constant contact with them. A series of costly defences or settlements could affect the general level of premiums, or even drive the underwriters out of the market altogether. In these circumstances, it would be surprising to find the brokers advising any course of action in opposition to the views of the underwriters. But I would emphasise that this is my personal assessment and opinion.

3.4.1 What are 'circumstances'?

Architects become aware of the possibility of a claim in many different ways. The awareness may strike terror in their hearts, it may create a burning resentment or a guilty conscience, or they may not even recognise it as a potential claim. As a general rule, any knowledge of a defect in a building is knowledge of a potential claim — whether or not anybody else yet knows of it. Tenders coming in above budget may well presage a claim — if only in response to an account for abortive fees. Contractor's claims for extension of time because of late supply of information could well finish up as a claim from a client.

If you think that you have the possibility of a claim, get out your policy and read it. In particular, check the conditions relating to notification, and if you are not obliged to notify at this stage, make a note to do so before renewal. A question insurers will ask with compelling insistency after notification is, 'When did you first become aware of this problem?'. If you have recently changed insurers and they can establish that you were aware before you insured with them, they will be quite justified in repudiating liability. If you have been continuously insured by the same office, the position may be not quite so bad — but you may be limited to the cover you had on the earlier policy.

If you have a broker, discuss the problem with him, and ask him to make the notification. Depending on the size and nature of the problem, insurers have

four courses open to them: to settle; to fight; to delay; to hope the problem will
go away.

First and foremost, their interest is to be rid of the situation as cheaply as
possible. The architect's interest is more complex. He will certainly want the
matter disposed of within the limits of his cover. He will probably want to
preserve a relationship with his client. He certainly will not want his reputation with other clients and the world at large to be tarnished. And he too
would like the matter disposed of quickly, if possible, and with as little
expenditure of time and effort on his part as possible.

Insofar as the insurers have any control over the progress of a claim, they will
want to know as much as possible about the background and the available
evidence. They may ask you to send them copies of relevant documents or, if the
claim is likely to be a big one, they may send an assessor to your office to look
through your files himself. Unless the claim is one which has emerged from the
mists of the past, they will normally wish for the architect to carry on a normal
relationship with his client while they give advice on the precise wording of
any correspondence related to the matter in dispute. They will probably make
an internal assessment of the magnitude of their risk, and try to set a sum
against their possible exposure. If they have only been notified of 'circumstances', it is unlikely that at this stage they will go to the expense of appointing independent experts, but almost certainly they will appoint solicitors to act
on your behalf. Building claims are a very specialised field, and there are not
many firms with the necessary expertise and experience. The few who specialise
in this field deal with the greater bulk of the cases, and the probability is that all
the significant features in your own case will be recognised by them as typical
and commonplace.

3.4.2 The need for patience

It is seldom to the advantage of the insurers to take the initiative in a claim
situation. However much the architect would like the matter cleared up and out
of the way as quickly as possible, the insurers almost invariably will adopt a low
profile, leaving it to the claimant to make the running. While this may be
extremely frustrating for the target of the claim, it is quite understandable from
the insurers' point of view. As the claimant begins to assemble his case, he may
become aware of complexities that he had not originally realised. While his
claim may be quite genuine and his loss very real, he may also recognise the
traps, pitfalls, and expense of litigation, and either drop his claim or offer to
settle on reasonable terms. He will be advised by his own solicitors of costs
which he will not be able to recoup and of the delays inherent in the legal
process. Probably less than half of all 'notifications' actually become formal
claims or threats of claims, and while it may take some considerable while —
years in most cases — for a notification actually to die and be written off,
insurers have great patience and are prepared to wait indefinitely for such an
advantageous outcome.

It is extremely rare for underwriters to agree to any settlement in advance of a
formal claim. Under the terms of the standard PI policy, they are only obliged
to reimburse you for sums which you are legally obliged to pay, and an offer

by a claimant to settle is usually taken as a sign of weakness in his actual case. By a similar token, any offer from the architect's side to settle usually acts to stiffen the resolve of the claimant.

3.4.3 The progress of a claim

Even the service of a writ, together with a statement of claim, may not move matters very far forward. It is only the first and necessary step by the claimant in setting out his claim, and writs tend always to be couched in the most general and all-embracing terms, very often omitting the most significant feature of all — the amount of the claim.

It is probable at this stage that underwriters will appoint 'experts' to investigate technical aspects of the claim, to indicate where blame might properly reside, and to advise on the possible responsibility of other parties. The experts will wish to inspect the affected building and go through all the drawings and documentation on the project. In the meantime, what can only be likened to a game of tennis is in progress as the lawyers ask each other for greater detail of the claim and of the defence to it. The process of further and better particulars, the preparation and responding to of Scott schedules, is seemingly endless and involves all parties in an inordinate expenditure of time and expense.

The Scott schedule figures in virtually all building claims and is a method of analysing a claim into its various components. Usually of double-page width and many pages in length, it describes each defective item, the act of negligence alleged to have brought it about, the remedial work necessary, the cost of the remedial work, and the amount claimed in respect of it from the defendant or defendants. It is probably during the preparation of the Scott Schedule that the claimant becomes aware of the shortcomings in his case and, more particularly, that he is not going to win in respect of every item.

It is only after the delivery of the Scott schedule and the disclosure by the other side of all the documentation on which they are relying that the defence is really in a position to contemplate settlement.

There are two ways of going about the settlement of a claim: to sit round a table, or to pay into court.

No settlement will be made or proposed without the architect's agreement. I will return to that point.

3.4.4 Paying into court

Paying into court is a process whereby the defendant, or the lawyers on his behalf, deposit with the court a sum of money. The claimant has the choice of taking that money out in settlement of his claim, or leaving it there and proceeding with the litigation. If he takes the money out, then that is the end of the matter, but if he decides to continue with the suit and is finally awarded less than the money paid into court, then he has to bear his own costs from the time the money was paid in. Similarly, if he is awarded more than the amount paid in, then the defendant will be responsible for the claimant's costs right through to the end of the trial.

So 'paying in' is a matter of some moment for the defence and requires the most careful judgement. Obviously they do not wish to pay in too much, because the claimant will take the money and run, but if they pay in too little, their action will have achieved nothing. At this stage, the tennis players have retired to the clubhouse and are playing poker.

3.4.5 Agreeing to settle

The alternative to 'paying in' is to sit around the table, but in multi–defendant cases, this is by no means easy to achieve, nor is there any certainty that a satisfactory compromise will emerge. That sort of settlement is usually reserved for the 'steps of the court', when the costs of the trial are looming so large in the minds of all the parties that a new spirit of urgency enters their deliberations. I wrote earlier that any settlement has to be with the consent of the defendant. It sometimes happens, particularly where the claim is a comparatively small one, that it is in the interests of the underwriters to settle rather than to fight, even though there may be a valid defence. Most policies give the defendant the right to insist that a claim is defended if an independent Queen's Counsel advises that there is a valid defence. The defendant, or for that matter the insurers, may invoke the QC clause at any time.

Unfortunately, it is not as easy as that. If you force your insurers to defend a claim that they would rather settle and, as a result, they are put to a great deal more expense, then you will not have endeared yourself to them. This may be reflected in the terms offered at the next renewal of your policy, or it may even result in a refusal to renew at all. Even if you approve the settlement, it may well be reflected in your renewal terms, and I have already quoted the case of the architect who, having approved a settlement, found himself with an uninsured potential risk, running into millions of pounds, at his next renewal. Whether he could have done anything about this at all is a matter of conjecture, but it is not unreasonable, if you think that your insurers are settling for their own benefit, to attempt to reach some understanding with them over renewal terms before you give your consent to the settlement. This is something best handled by your broker; if he feels unable to deal with it, discuss it with your own private solicitor.

Regrettably, your position is not a strong one, because your insurance contract is an annual one and your underwriters are free agents. If they do not want to insure you, there is no power on earth that can make them. The one point in your favour is that, having paid out on a claim for you, your insurers will generally want to retain the opportunity to recoup at least part of their loss through your future business.

3.4.6 Notification and disclosure

Although policies may be written differently in detail, they are all pretty specific about the need for notification. It is no use waiting until you have damages awarded against you in court and then telling your insurers about it. Nor is it particularly sensible to agree with a client that you have made a mistake and that you will pay for the remedial work yourself. By all means do so if you wish, but don't expect your insurers to reimburse you.

There are two kinds of notification, and it is as well to understand the difference. On your proposal form there will be a question regarding 'any circumstances of which you are aware that might give rise to a claim'. Faced with the fatuity of that question, I am always tempted to send the insurers all our drawings and files and say that these are all circumstances that might give rise to a claim. However, there will be occasions on which you will be aware of circumstances; certainly if you have been made aware of them by third parties, either orally or in writing, then disclose them. If you fail to do so and later have cause to advise your insurers of a potential claim, you may be without cover.

A few years ago, a client contacted me regarding a building that had been completed some years previously. He said that the ground floor walls were unstable and 'waving in the breeze'. I duly visited the site with the engineer, observed that the walls clearly were not waving in the breeze, had all the calculations checked, came to the conclusion that there was nothing amiss, and so advised the building owner. Privately, I was also reassured that if there was anything wrong, it would be in the engineer's court. And that was that.

Nine months later I received another letter from the building owner, saying that he had ordered remedial works costing £100,000 and he didn't think his company should have to pay. Still no claim, you note, but I decided to ask my brokers to notify the insurers as a prudent precaution. The insurers duly sent an assessor to see me to get further details; so having explained the background, I handed him the file, which he skipped lightly through and then departed. Two or three days later my very agitated broker was on the phone with disturbing tidings. The insurers were invalidating my insurance for 'non-disclosure'.

'What the hell are you talking about?', I demanded.

'You didn't tell them about the letter you got last year about the "walls waving in the breeze".'

'But that wasn't a claim — and the walls were not waving in the breeze.'

'No. But when you completed your renewal proposal in February, you should have disclosed it. That was a circumstance of which you were aware that might give rise to a claim.'

According to my broker, the insurers were prepared to reinstate my insurance on payment of an additional premium, but they would still repudiate liability in respect of the particular problem of which I had just notified them.

Needless to say, the matter did not end there, and eventually the insurers agreed to reinstate without penalty and to take the problem under their cover. In the event, no claim materialised, but I had learnt several very valuable lessons.

The point to bear in mind is that, while your policy may require you only to notify an actual claim or a specific threat of a claim during the currency of the policy, at renewal you must open up fully and honestly about all those doubtful matters which may give rise to a claim. I use the word 'may', but policies are worded differently, and the differences can be significant. There is a world of difference between 'may', 'might', 'likely to', and you are entitled to make a judgement on whether any particular circumstances should be disclosed under your particular policy.

Architects, understandably, have a reluctance to advise their insurers every time a query arises and believe, with whatever foundation, that these notification are a black mark on their policy and may affect their renewal terms. This may even be the case, although my own experience is that renewal terms are affected only by the existence of actual claims. But in truth, one has no choice in the matter. If you do not disclose, you may have a lower premium — but no cover when you want it.

Brokers who specialise in professional indemnity insurance report that they constantly have to deal with claims where the first indication of a problem is the writ served by an irate claimant. They then discover that the problem has been dragging on for months or years, with the architect attempting to deal with it from his own resources. What has happened is that the architect has assessed the problem as trivial or minor and probably of less value than his excess. Having, and wanting to preserve, the excellent relationship he has with his client, he has bent over backwards to sort the problem out. But the problem has grown, the builder has proved unco-operative, the client has lost patience (and money), and suddenly the egg has hit the fan!

What happens next will depend on a number of factors — not least, the relationship that has been established between the architect and his insurers. If the policy is a new one and the problem was not disclosed on the first proposal, then the chances are that the insurers will repudiate liability. If there is a long-standing relationship, then the insurers may take a more relaxed view and maintain cover, but at the limit of indemnity purchased in the year when the notification should have been made.

Perhaps the trickiest situation to deal with is the occasion when the architect is aware that he has been negligent — but his client is blissfully unaware. The architect may be able to remedy the defect at some cost. If he fails to do so, the damage may later be considerably more and then the client might discover the facts and claim. Is the architect covered? This may depend as much on the facts of the case as the actual wording of the policy.

At the time of writing, the ABS Insurance Agency has changed its underwriters, and a significant change in policy wording now requires notification as soon as reasonably possible after the discovery of an error that is likely to give rise to a claim.

Bearing in mind that the policy is an annual contract, the wording generally provides cover at any later date in respect of any matter notified in the policy year. So it may well be in the insurers' interest to support you in advance of any claim, even though they may have no strict liability to do so. Certainly it is worth talking to them about it.

There is one cardinal rule in dealing with your insurers: come clean. However great the temptation to delay telling them something, or to conceal something, resist it. Insurers are in the business of making money, and the easiest way to make money is to take the premiums and then not have to pay out. Only a fool will pay his premium and then give his insurers grounds on which to repudiate liability or invalidate the insurance.

1 The interests of insurer and insured are not identical and may be directly opposed. You may need help, so speak to your broker, solicitor, or institute.

2 Learn to recognise 'circumstances that may give rise to a claim'. If you need to notify, then for goodness sake do so.

3 Unless you have very good reasons, don't push your insurers to speed up progress. Generally they know what they're doing, and it seldom pays the defendant to make the running.

4 If your insurers want to settle even though there is a good defence, they cannot do so without your consent. If they are settling purely for their own advantage, they have no claim on your excess. But be prepared for a refusal to renew.

5 Check your policy wording on 'notification' and always comply with the requirement.

6 Whatever the embarrassment, come clean with your insurers and deal honestly with them. When you are in trouble, the last thing you want is a dispute with your insurers over your own lack of good faith.

3.5 Protecting your retirement

There are few more distressing sights than that of a man who, having worked hard and honourably through his life and provided diligently, if modestly, for his old age, being pursued through the courts and towards penury or worse in his declining years. With the law on liability as it stands today, such cases are becoming increasingly common, and at the RIBA I have a growing file of letters from distressed retired architects which would disabuse even the most naive of any faith or belief in British justice.

These cases all seem to fall into a common pattern, and a typical letter runs as follows.

Dear Sir

I think your members ought to know about a problem I have. I am 75 years old [or 80, or 85] and I was in practice from 1920 until I retired in 1965. I kept up my professional indemnity insurance until 1972, when I allowed it to lapse in the belief that I could no longer be sued in respect of my work in practice.

A few months ago, I received a letter from a firm of solicitors advising me that a building I designed in 1962 [or 1952] had suffered subsidence [or cracking, or leaking], the damage had been repaired [often at a cost exceeding the original

building cost], and that their clients (of whom I had never heard) were holding me responsible. Would I please write agreeing my liability [or advise them
of my insurers].

Since my retirement, I have lived in a small flat, and my capital is invested to
provide a supplement to my state pension. Even the costs of defending this
claim will seriously deplete my retirement fund. The builder, who was probably
at fault, no longer exists, and the local authority, which is being sued, intends to
defend the case and has said they will seek a contribution from me if I am not
named as a defendant.

I no longer have my practice records, my wife became so distressed that she had
a heart attack and is now in hospital, and I am at my wit's end. Can you help
me? I have been a member of the RIBA for 48 years.
Yours faithfully

Every one of the circumstances in the above composite letter has appeared in
one or more letters on my file, and each letter sets off my sense of outrage, which
nowadays is admittedly on a pretty short fuse.

The ability of the RIBA to assist in these cases is very limited. Proposals were
made some years ago to establish a defence fund for these hard-luck cases — but
so far nothing has been done. In the well publicised case of Bertram Carter, 85
years of age and in poor health, representations to the claimants, Dr
Barnardo's, elicited an assurance that they would not proceed against him —
but that if any other defendant joined him in for contribution, they could do
nothing about it. As most claimants nowadays tend to be institutions, public
authorities, or insurance companies, representations may sometimes be
effective, but there is no guarantee.

3.5.1 Indemnity from continuing partners

So what steps should a retiring practitioner take to avoid, so far as possible, this
kind of catastrophe? Architects who practise in partnership are able to protect
themselves to some extent by obtaining an indemnity from the remaining
partners, and this is common procedure. But the terms of the indemnity need to
be carefully drawn if they are not going to provide merely the illusion rather
than the reality.

The most common indemnity will be 'in respect of the retired member's professional work while he was a member of the practice'. This is rather less than the
protection he may have had while he was a member of the practice, in that the
practice policy probably covered the partners retroactively for all their professional work, including that before the partnership was formed or before a
particular partner joined.

A better form of protection is for the retired partner to continue to be covered by
the practice policy in exactly the same terms as previously. Most standard
policy wording covers this as 'all present and previous partners of the
practice'. The problem faced by a retired partner is that he has no way of
ensuring that the partnership will continue in being, or that the remaining
partners will insure adequately (or at all), or that, in the event of inadequate
insurance, he will know about it in time to take avoiding action.

Times change, and by inadvertence or design, a retired partner may well find he is not covered as he thought. So an important factor in any retirement agreement should be an obligation to notify any change in the circumstances of the practice, any claims that might exceed the amount of indemnity, and so on. The time to make these arrangements is not at retirement, but on setting up or joining a partnership. The obligations of remaining partners to retired partners should be clearly spelt out from the outset and, in the interests of all parties, updated in the light of any changes in the law as time passes. Particularly does this apply if the form of the practice changes.

I have discussed this point with the senior partner of a large firm where they are considering changing to a limited liability structure. In limited liability, the joint and several liability of partners does not apply, so there is little incentive to carry the burden of a retired partner — an additional cost which effectively is borne by the young for the benefit of the old. One of the advantages of practising in limited liability is that the practice itself can 'cut off the tail' of past work carried out by previous partners. To take on the burden of indemnities given by one or more of the members of the firms to past partners does, to some extent, frustrate this advantage — and strictly speaking could even be held to be not in the interest of the company.

So given foresight, a good lawyer, and a stable practice that is not going to change its form, disappear, or invalidate its insurance, a retiring partner can organise reasonable protection for himself — up to a point. Beyond that point, he may still be exposed, and how to deal with that exposure I deal with later.

3.5.2 The problem of the sole principal
There are in the United Kingdom something in excess of 2,500 practices with a total complement of one or two 'technical staff including partners' — one-man bands. How can a sole principal, lone practitioner, or one-man band ever retire in safety or even die with any peace of mind that his widow may not be deprived of the competence he has left her? Philosophers or cynics might say that the only sure thing in life is death; but there are steps that can be taken to remove the very worst hazards of liability in retirement. These are examined generally below, but the best advice I can give is to consult a good lawyer when you make plans for your retirement. But make sure it is a lawyer who is truly experienced in the problems of architects' liability. There are not many of them around. Most lawyers I talk to seem to have very little idea of the problems of the construction professions.

3.5.3 Sell your practice
For a multitude of reasons, many practitioners do not actually retire at all. They allow their professional activity slowly to peter out until one day there is no work to do — and they have retired. The tired remains of a one-man practice may not, in fact, be worth very much in money terms, but client contacts and a bit of goodwill are usually worth something. If you can sell your practice for no more than an undertaking to insure your liability, you may have done a good deal. Do not receive the money yourself. Arrange that the acquiring firm covers your liability in respect of past work within their PI insurance. You will

then be in a very similar position to that of an architect retiring from a partnership, referred to earlier in this chapter.

3.5.4 Purchase run-off insurance
A problem many retired practitioners come up against is that, in retirement, their premiums cease to be tax-deductible. But a single premium expended in the final year of practice is a business expense and could reduce your tax liability. So try to negotiate a fairly long period of run-off insurance for a single premium — and make certain that it is non-cancellable.

Run-off insurance premiums reduce annually, and a good broker may be able to negotiate a longer period than the three years now generally available. It may be difficult to make a good estimate of the amount of cover you will require, but try to be realistic. It is with some regret I have to tell you that insurers are becoming less and less willing to underwrite run-off cover.

Few retired practitioners will be able to afford even reduced premiums if, happily, they enjoy long retirement, so the day may come when you will be without cover. In this condition of maximum vulnerability, what should one do?

3.5.5 Remove yourself from the battlefield
To some, retirement to Majorca or the Cayman Islands may have its attractions. If so, bon voyage! With no exchange controls, removal of yourself and your assets from within the jurisdiction of the courts is perhaps the simplest answer to the whole problem; and the weather is better.

3.5.6 Remove your assets from the jurisdiction of the courts
Emigration is not attractive to all. The lifelong dream of a cottage in the Cotswolds is too big a sacrifice even for the sake of peace of mind. But if you do plan to spend your retirement in the UK, there is no reason why your assets and retirement fund should be hostage. A number of courses are open to you, all admittedly with drawbacks, and each man has his own order of priorities.

There are basic precautions, such as having your wife own the roof over your head. If you have no wife, you may be better off in rented accommodation. There are schemes available now whereby you can sell your home to an institution, with vacant possession on the death of yourself and wife. The proceeds of the sale can be invested for you in the purchase of an annuity.

If you are intending to bequeath your assets to your family, it may be possible to establish a family trust. See an expert, or you may end up like King Lear, who also had problems in his retirement. The very worst thing you can do is to own stocks and shares and live off the income.

3.5.7 Purchase 'disaster' insurance
There is one further way to protect your assets against a liability assault, and that is a limited indemnity insurance, which merely protects the value of your assets. Not yet widely available, it is cheapest for those practitioners who have retired from a partnership or otherwise arranged for their liability to be borne by others. In the event that those arrangements break down for any reason, then the claimant has a choice. He can settle his claim for no more than the

Remove yourself from the battlefield

value of the insurance, or he can pursue you through the courts in the knowledge that, whatever he is awarded, he cannot obtain more, even by making you bankrupt. Faced with the choice, any claimant will take the insurance money and run.

3.5.8 Purchase litigation insurance

Yet another way of discouraging assaults on your retirement fund is to take out legal defence insurance. Such a policy will indemnify you for your costs in defending a lawsuit but not against any damages that may be awarded against you. Here the claimant is, as they say, 'on to a black eye to nothing'. He knows he will be put to the trouble and expense of a contested lawsuit in which your costs are assured, but where even if he wins he may be able to obtain very little.

3.5.9 Protect your estate

Owen Luder's tale about the descendants of Christopher Wren being sued if St Paul's Cathedral develops a fault is a classic hyperbole based in solid fact. It is a chilling thought that one can in English law actually be sued for a personal offence — negligence — when one is no longer around to defend either one's good name or the provision one has made for one's widow and orphans. This is something that affects not only retired and ageing practitioners: the reaper arrives uninvited and is no respecter of birthdays. An insurance contract is renewable annually, and how many PI policies are renewed or replaced by some other protection on the death of the principal? Far be it from me to suggest that there is a legion of family lawyers who should be sued for negligence for failing to advise widows on the dangers of post-mortem claims. The fact that assaults on the estates of deceased architects are comparatively rare is beside the point — they do occur.

There was a time when I fondly believed that these circumstances arose only when the action in negligence had been commenced before the death of the architect. In a sense, that would have been understandable, if only because contemplation of a writ for damages can have a dramatically unsettling effect on the health of an octogenarian, and it would be grossly unjust to a claimant to bar his action only because his taking it might result in the death of the defendant. That might sound a little callous, and indeed there is, as I have subsequently discovered, no need for a claimant to precipitate the death of his target by rushing around and serving the writ before the ageing architect departs this place. To preserve his conscience, and subject to the Statute of Limitations, he can wait for the architect to die and then serve the writ on the estate. And you thought that all humanity had gone from commerce!

At a conference in 1982, a solicitor much involved in the affairs of architects opined that the estate of an architect was probably secure from assault a year after his death. John Edwards, managing director of the ABS Insurance Agency, which covers more than half of the profession for PI, disagreed. He was dealing with a case where a widow was defending her husband's estate 12 years after his death. Such a conflict of views requires clarification. A claimant's ability to sue a deceased architect's estate seems to depend on his ability to identify it. Most estates become dissipated, or transformed, very shortly after the grant of probate or letters of administration, and once that happens, the potential claimant has a difficulty. But it is not unknown — indeed it is very common — for an estate (or some part of it), to be left in trust for the benefit of the widow in her lifetime and then to children or other legatees. Estates left in trust are identifiable and accordingly are valid targets. Again, I am way outside the sphere of any knowledge or expertise I may have — discuss your will with your lawyer and draw his attention to these dangers.

Even the comparatively short period between death and probate should be protected in some way against the lapsing of PI insurance. Again, this is a point to discuss with your lawyer and insurance broker if you are a sole practitioner. It is a condemnation of our legal system and our society that this chapter had to be written at all. We really ought to be able to arrange our affairs in such a way that, in retirement and after death, practitioners are secure from assault. It is bad enough that one works under a spectre of legal assault throughout one's working life. It is unpleasant, but it is possible to take defensive measures, with a fair possibility of being able to find the money to pay for them. After retirement, everything changes. Incomes are usually much reduced, earning capacity may have disappeared, physical power to defend oneself is diminished, yet vulnerability to assault remains. It is hardly cricket. Perhaps we could persuade the League Against Cruel Sports to take up the case.

Checklist: Protecting your retirement

---

1   Arrange if you possibly can for succession in your practice with an obligation to insure your liability.

---

2   Purchase the best run-off insurance you can get in the last year of practice, when the premium will be tax-deductible.

---

3   Maintain your run-off insurance as long as possible.

---

4   Remove yourself from the jurisdiction of the courts.

---

5   Remove your assets from the jurisdiction of the courts by putting them in your spouse's name or in trust, or by investing them, or by purchasing an annuity with your capital.

---

6   Purchase litigation insurance.

---

7   Purchase 'disaster' insurance to the value of your estate.

---

8   Do not leave your estate in trust on your death. If it is identifiable, then it is vulnerable.

3.6 Practising as a limited liability company

In 1981, the Royal Institute of British Architects changed its Code of Conduct to permit its members to practise architecture in the form of companies with limited liability. As one of those who opposed that and other changes to the code, with more vigour than ultimate success, I have to declare an interest and state that I do not approve of practising in limited liability for a number of reasons concerned with my concept of professionalism — and, incidentally, because I believe it may actually increase one's vulnerability to claims.

The changes in the code followed a poll of the entire membership of the RIBA and, on most of the issues that the members voted on, the pros and antis were fairly equally divided. But on two issues, the decisions were made by the two-thirds majority necessary to mandate the Institute to give effect to the decisions of the poll. The membership refused to permit advertising, but insisted that members be allowed to practise in limited liability. From those two votes, one could only draw the conclusion that the profession was not interested so much in commercialising itself as in providing a degree of protection against the unlimited liability, both in amount and over time, to which the profession is currently subject. It was perfectly clear at the time that many members felt that the ability to limit their liability in company structure was a complete answer to their problems on liability. The institute issued a long practice note setting out the legal position, from which it is quite clear that the protection afforded by this sort of structure is by no means complete.

While this book is no place for a treatise on company law, there is so much mis-understanding over what is meant by limited liability that this chapter has been written in the hope that it will clear the air.

3.6.1 What is a company?

A company is a corporate entity in its own right. It exists and may own assets, acquire debts, enter into contracts, employ staff — in fact a company may do most things that can be done by an individual. It can cease to exist only by a process of liquidation. A company may have a nominal capital of £100 or £1m, but the amount is immaterial: it is the capital that is issued and paid up which is of interest to the outside world.

The whole of the assets of the company is represented by the issued and paid-up shares. If a company is worth £1m but has issued only two £1 shares, then those two shares will each be worth £½m. Conversely, if it has issued 10,000 £1 shares, but has net assets worth £100, then each share will only be worth 1p.

3.6.2 Paid-up capital

It is usual, but by no means obligatory, when starting up a company to issue capital which relates fairly closely to the asset value of the company. Accordingly, if you are going to convert your unlimited practice into a limited company and you estimate the net asset value of your practice at £10,000, it would be reasonable to establish a company with an issued and paid-up share capital of £10,000 divided into 10,000 shares with a nominal value of £1 each. If you are a sole principal, you may issue all but one of the shares to yourself, or if you have a partner, you could have 5,000 shares each. You will note that the shares are issued and fully paid up. The shares were paid for by transferring to the company the ownership of personal assets worth £10,000, they being the net asset value of your previously privately owned practice. As your shares are fully paid up, you have fully discharged any liability you may have to creditors of the company. If the company falls on hard times and cannot pay its bills, then the creditors of the company cannot call upon the shareholders to make good any deficit. Your liability is limited to the paid-up value of your shares. The creditors have to content themselves with whatever may be salvaged from the assets of the company.

However, while your house or your private fortune (if you have one) may be safe from the depradations of your creditors, the company's assets will all be gone. If a receiver is appointed, he will call in all outstanding fees, realise all your fixed assets, and so on. It may be possible to protect your fixed assets through the medium of a service company, but a commercial disaster is still a commercial disaster, and you may be having to start your practice again from scratch.

3.6.3 Personal guarantees
If you are looking for the normal commercial protection of limited liability, here is a word of warning to you: never sign a personal guarantee. This may be easier said than done, because if you rent your premises as a private company, it is very common for the landlord to insist on the personal guarantees of the directors. You may well find that you have a continuing liability for the rent of your premises even when you have no practice to house in them.

3.6.4 The protection of limited liability
How does the commercial protection of limited liability affect the issue of professional liability?

First and foremost, the contract for the supply of professional service is between the company and the client. This means that if an architectural error is committed, it is committed by the company and it is the company that is in breach of contract. Hence, the first remedy by the damaged party is against the company. Now it is all very well to say to your aggrieved client, 'OK, sue me. We are only a £1,000 company, and you can't get what isn't there!'. The fact of the matter is that he probably will sue you and, if you do not have adequate insurance, will put your company into liquidation. He will have a claim on the assets of the company and they may by then be worth far more than the nominal £1,000 paid-up capital that shows in the company particulars. I said earlier that practising in limited liability might render you more liable to claims, and certainly there is less inhibition against suing an impersonal entity like a company than against actually naming the friendly neighbourhood architect. So the prudent company and its directors, who wish to protect the company's assets, will in any event insure against claims for professional negligence. There is at the present time no indication that there will be a difference in the premiums payable by companies and by those architects practising as individuals or in unlimited-liability company structure.

3.6.5 The claimant's remedy in tort
If it is a fact that the company has no assets and no insurance, the aggrieved

client may well feel that he has been set up for a raw deal. In that case, he may look round for some other remedy. He has a remedy in tort against any employee of the company who he can actually identify as having been the cause of his damage. Architecture is an activity in which it is difficult to hide. Particularly in small practices, it is not at all difficult to identify the person actually responsible for the negligent action. It is not good enough for a director or an employee of a company to say that his duty is to the company alone. The law will not have that: the law will insist that he has a duty of care to those who, in his reasonable contemplation, might be damaged by his actions. So, company or not, if a client is going to serve a writ on the practice, he will, if it is humanly possible also serve a writ for damages in tort against whomever he can identify as being the perpetrator of his downfall. The main advantage here in practising as a company is that there is no joint and several responsibility of the proprietors. The claimant has to identify the individual, and he alone is the responsible party. In most partnerships, a successful suit against one parter would be considered as a disaster for them all, whatever the legal position.

I have to say that the courts are increasingly taking a view that extends the liability in tort in many directions. The interpretations seem to be becoming looser, and the whole of the law seems to be directed to ensuring that the damaged party receives his compensation. So practice in limited liability will not help you if you can be identified as the negligent party.

It may be possible so to organise your practice that you as a director and shareholder are never identified as being responsible for anything, but — particularly in the case of the sole principal — this does present severe practical difficulties.

3.6.6 Ensure that the company policy covers individuals

If, as an architect practising in limited liability, you are sued in tort, you are sued as an individual. If your company has taken out insurance against its own liability, unless you have specifically required that your personal liability be covered at the same time, then you will be unprotected, and your personal wealth will be hostage to the directions of the court. You should not assume that the company's policy automatically covers its directors or employees. It may include a waiver of its rights of subrogation against directors and employees, but that is not the same thing as directly protecting those directors and employees.

Because the whole concept of professional practice in limited liability is so new, there is as yet no case law to quote so far as architects are concerned. But as an indication of the way in which the judiciary is thinking, it is worth looking at the case where an architect engaged by a limited company sued the individual directors for fees and won his case. The view of the court was that the directors were acting in partnership with the limited company and so the court held the individuals liable. Turn that case on its head and you will see that the architect who practises in limited liability to avoid his proper professional responsibilities under the law will probably receive scant protection from the law when it comes to the crunch.

There are good, valid, and professionally ethical reasons for wishing to practise

under the umbrella of limited liability. They are primarily concerned with the
structure of practice and the mobility and flexibility of the principals within
the firm. Most often, the decision on whether to practise in limited liability will
relate to matters of taxation, profit sharing, and so on. Given good reasons for
practising in limited liability, then there are some advantages, notably the
avoidance of joint and several responsibility where one of the principals has
been delinquent and has been sued in tort. To practise in limited liability
successfully and with responsibility, it is still necessary to maintain professional
indemnity insurance to guard your client against the defects of your practice,
at least as much as for any other reason.

Finally, should you change from partnership to limited liability company,
your responsibility and liability in respect of the work you carried out under the
former structure remain with you perpetually. Make sure they are covered.

Checklist: Limited liability

1   Limited liability is no substitute for responsible insurance.

2   Limited liability may protect your personal fortune — but not the assets of
the practice unless they are owned by another corporate entity.

3   Individuals within the company may still be sued in tort if identifiable.

4   There is no joint and several liability as between the shareholders or
directors.

5   If you change the form of your practice, you are still personally liable for the
work you carried out in partnership.

6   The protection afforded by limited liability, especially in very small
practices, may be largely illusory. It was designed to protect the individual
against the normal hazards of commercial enterprise. An architect's
professional liability is a more complex matter, and there are no certain routes
to safety.

3.7 Going bare

Whenever the subject of professional liability is discussed, somebody will point
to the example of professional practitioners in the United States who have
adopted the device of divesting themselves of their assets, or 'going bare'. It is
an undeniable fact that, if you are without means or assets, nobody in his right
mind, even supported by legal aid, is going to sue you. But going bare is easier
said than done, particularly if you wish to spend your retirement living on
something rather better than a state pension.

The classic method of 'going bare' is to put the whole of one's assets into one's
wife's name. Provided that this is a long-standing arrangement and that the

Going bare

assets have been transferred at least two years before you were aware of a claim against you, then they will probably be safe. Well, they will be safe from the claimant, but what you do if your wife decides to increase the ever-rising divorce statistics is another question, as also is the distressing circumstance of the wife who, owning all the assets, predeceases her husband.

I have not investigated all the ways which may be open to one to divest oneself of assets, or at any rate to remove them sufficiently from the grasp of claimants. I am sure that with the advice of a good lawyer, it can be done quite effectively, but what the architect's proclaimed penury does for his reputation as a professional practitioner is something else again, and it is unlikely to inspire the trust and respect of a potential client. It is true that it has worked in the United States, particularly for doctors, but doctors are in exceptional demand in the United States, certainly more so than architects in the United Kingdom. Going bare may have its attractions for some, but I suspect that its appeal is limited to a very tiny minority.

3.8 The liability of salaried staff

Only a few years ago, it would not have occurred to anyone to write on such an unlikely topic as this. There was a general presumption that the employer was responsible for the acts of his employees, so why worry? Indeed, an employer does have what is known in law as a vicarious liability for the actions of his staff — but that only means that a claimant may, if he wishes, sue the employer rather than pursue the employee. It does not absolve the salaried employee from the consequence of his own acts.

3.8.1 Changes in public attitudes

Subtle changes in public attitudes, and in the nature and status of salaried employment, have brought about a need for salaried employees to look much more closely at their potential liabilities, and to take such steps as are open to them to reduce their exposure. Particularly in architecture, and certainly more so than in most other professions, employment as a qualified professional is no longer inevitably a stepping-stone to partnership or the establishment of one's own practice. Increasingly, salaried employment may be a total professional career. Generally, that career will be spent in the public sector or in private practice, but in all sides of industry and commerce, salaried architects are occupying appointments wherein they are totally responsible for major building projects or construction programmes. They exercise their professional skills responsibly and without supervision.

3.8.2 The vulnerability of the project architect

Within both public and private practice, there is constant pressure for this responsibility to be acknowledged and published. Read the write-ups in the professional press in which every one gives credit, not only to the firm or organisation primarily responsible, but also to the project architect and sometimes even the entire project team.

However, it is not the mere knowledge of the employee's responsibility that places him in jeopardy. It is that he may be the only, or most likely, target of a claimant. A damaged party will always seek advice. Given that he has truly suffered damage from causes that may be actionable, a prudent lawyer will select his target defendants with some care.

Forgetting for a moment the poor claimant, the lawyer himself will want to be satisfied that, win or lose, he will receive payment for his labours. He certainly stands a better chance of being paid if, having won, the claimant actually receives his damages and costs. Pyrrhic victories are of even less benefit to the lawyers than they are to the principal contestants, who at least have the personal satisfaction of having won their point.

Selecting a target or targets may not be an easy task. With liability unlimited in time, many years may have passed since the negligent act that caused the damage. The original firm may no longer exist, or its principals may be retired and without means or insurance. With architects now permitted to practise as limited liability companies, the firm may have liquidated long since, and the same may apply where the architect was employed by a development company or industrial concern.

Further, not all architect principals are wealthy men — indeed, most would claim to earn less than senior employees, and the RIBA's own statistics add some credence to the claim. In *Eames* v *North London Estates* (referred to above), the architect principal had no insurance and little wealth. Had he been the sole defendant, the claimants would have received little for their trouble.

So the claimant's lawyer can be forgiven for looking to see whether responsibility can be placed on some individual or body with the means to pay. Provided he has the means, who better than the 'project architect'? Easily identified, his name published in the journals and appearing on drawings, site minutes, instructions, and perhaps even certificates, he may deny negligence but he cannot easily repudiate responsibility. In the years that have elapsed since the project architect executed that particular ill-fated project, much may have changed in his own circumstances. He may well have substantial assets, a house, a car (or two), savings not protected in a pension fund. It is quite likely that he may by now himself be a principal in practice, with considerable assets and a vital interest in remaining solvent. All this may be hostage if the lawyer directs the claim at him entirely or as a co-defendant. If it can be shown that it was his own negligent act that caused the defect, then damages will be awarded against him.

3.8.3 Exceeding one's authority

There are other ways in which salaried staff can find themselves at risk. An employee can be held responsible for his professional acts if they are beyond the remit given him by his employer. Indeed, a professionally qualified employee can even find himself liable to his employer for damage he causes by his unauthorised acts. Happily, such cases are extremely rare, if only because generally the principal realises he has only himself to blame.

3.8.4 The need for employees to exercise judgement

Perhaps the greatest hazard the employed architect faces is the conflict that may arise between his own professional judgement and the instructions he receives from his employer. In the same category is the architect working in conditions that do not permit him to perform properly his professional responsibilities. It is an unfortunate fact of life that some employers are too ready to pass the financial constraints of their practices on to the shoulders of their staff, without too much thought of the consequences. And let it be said that this is not confined to the private sector. In recent years, many local authorities, under pressure to cut expenditure, have butchered professional departments without concern or any conception of the way in which they have prejudiced their staffs in the performance of their professional tasks.

It is because the employee may not always be free to exercise his independent judgement that the concept of vicarious liability arose. Similarly, the law considers it against public policy for an employer to recover from an employee any damages he may have to pay to third parties. And that is why PI insurers waive their subrogatory rights against employees. They are not actually giving much away. Unless they could prove fraud or illegality (and that absolves them from their waiver), they could not succeed in such a claim in the courts.

The concept of vicarious liability is certainly a major protection for salaried staff — but it works only one way round. If, much later, an architect has to defend himself against a charge of negligence, he cannot plead vicarious liability. He could join his ex-employer into the case for contribution, except that if the ex-employer was available, the employee would probably not be in the case at all.

What steps can salaried staffs take to protect themselves? A recognition of the dangers is probably the best protection an employee can have. The biggest dangers arise from complacency that the liability is his employer's.

As I see it, there is one cardinal rule. The qualified professional must at all times exercise his own professional judgement. In law, his actions are subjected to the same scrutiny and standards of performance as are those of a principal. So he should never do under instruction or pressure any act which he would not do if he relied on his own judgement alone. Easier said than done, although most employers would recognise the justice of the stance. If an employee consistently feels that there is conflict between his judgment and that of his employer, he may in the final analysis have no alternative to resignation. The lesson to be learned here is that a job interview is a two-way exchange. Few job applicants take sufficient care to establish the reputation, attitudes, and philosophy of their potential employers. Maybe employers should present CVs as well as applicants!

3.8.5 The employer's insurance

The employer's insurance policy is the employee's first line of defence. It is completely proper for an employee to enquire about his employer's PI insurance arrangements. And it is prudent to include in the contract of employment a provision that the employer maintains suitable insurance — and undertakes to indemnify an employee after he has left his employment in respect of any liability incurred in the course of the engagement. Granted, the indemnity may be of value only while the ex-employer is around and has funds, but it is better than nothing.

If the employer is a limited liability company, the hazards are that much greater, and employees should absolutely insist on the maximum degree of protection that can be arranged. This should extend to an agreement by the employer to purchase run-off protection for an employee leaving the firm. There is one large development company with its own in-house architect's department which, to my knowledge, currently carries £5m cover, but has projects on hand to many times that value. Small wonder that I hear of the worries expressed by the chief architect and lesser staff about their position should there be a major claim and the design firm — a separate entity — be put into liquidation.* The best advice I can give to architects in this position is to go to a good lawyer and get the very best advice available.

3.8.6 Protect your assets

What else can be done? I have said before that a man of straw is not worth powder and shot. With the law in its present state, the salaried architect should take the same sensible precautions adopted by most practitioners, and try to protect his basic assets. To secure the family home is a basic precaution, and some might consider it a bounden duty. Protecting one's retirement fund is common procedure — but it does carry certain penalties in that the savings have to be tied up until retirement.

Perhaps most important of all, if he quits salaried employment and starts his own practice, he should attempt to buy retro-active contingency cover against claims arising from his work during employment. It should not be too expensive and will be a tax-deductible expense.

3.8.7 Conflicts of interest

An aspect of liability that needs to be considered closely is the position of architects in industry and commercial organisations where they are named as 'the architect' in building contracts and have to make quasi-judicial decisions in the administration of the contract.

I see a substantial conflict of interest arising in these cases, and the employed architect is exceptionally vulnerable to claims from contractors.

The pressures from his employer on the in-house architect can become burdensome and liable to affect his independent judgement, particularly if the financial condition of the employer is not entirely sound. If, as a result of the architect's failure to carry out his duties and obligations under the contract, the builder suffers loss that he cannot recover from the employer, then for a certainty he will seek redress from the architect. I doubt whether this risk can be covered by insurance or indemnity. The only sure defence is not to allow your professional judgement to be swayed by the pressures of your employment. Any contract of employment for an in-house professional should clearly set out

---

* *Since writing this, the company has indeed gone into liquidation.*

the professional's right and duty to exercise at all times his professional judgement. Then, if pressures are applied, you can at least quit without being sued for breach of contract — and you may have a claim against your employers for 'constructive dismissal'.

The role of the in-house professional is not an easy one to fulfill, although many commercial and industrial employers do acknowledge the wider responsibilities of their professional staffs. The difficulties are, in general, recognised in terms of higher earnings than for equivalent posts in conventional practice. This is fair enough as far as it goes, but it is small compensation if in the end you are faced with the choice of exposing yourself to claims or instant resignation. Care in the selection of your employer and in agreeing terms of contract is even more crucial for the architect in commerce than for his colleague in practice.

Checklist: Liability of salaried staff

1 Select your employer with care. Ensure that working conditions will permit the proper fulfillment of your professional responsibilities.

2 Always exercise your own professional judgement.

3 Ensure that your employer has 'suitable and adequate' insurance with a waiver of subrogation.

4 If you go into practice on your own account, purchase retro–active contingency cover.

5 Protect your personal assets.

6 In-house architects employed by commercial and industrial organisations should take legal advice on their contracts of employment, particularly in relation to the recognition of their professional and quasi–judicial responsibilities.

3.9 Self-employment and ghosting

Not all employed staff are salaried. This book is not the place to criticise those arrangements which have all the appearance of employment but may (or may not) in the eyes of the law be something quite different. It has to be assumed that professionally qualified people enter into their arrangements with their eyes open. It is to be hoped that the tax advantages of 'self-employment', contract work, or ghosting do not blind the participants to the very real penalties they may pay in other directions. First, it should perhaps be said that 'self-employment' which operates under the same disciplines and constraints as salaried employment is considered in law to be employment, with concomitant responsibilities for PAYE, National Insurance, and the like. If an architect enters into this kind of fictitious arrangement either as master or man, then both parties are breaking the law. It behoves both of them to guard carefully their other interests, among which their respective professional liabilities must loom large.

3.9.1 Self-employment

Let us deal only with genuine self-employment, by which I mean some kind of contract entered into by an architect for the supply of professional services to a fellow architect on the premises of that architect. What are his liabilities and how should he best arrange to protect himself? The essence of his situation is that of an architect in private practice, and his client is the architect for whom he is working. He has the same contractual duty to him as the principal archi-tect owes to the client on whose project the self-employed architect is working. In theory at least, his 'employer' could sue him for damages whenever he made a careless error or failed to bring a proper degree of skill or care to his work. That may be a little far-fetched, but it takes no stretch of the imagina-tion to foresee that kind of outcome if the employer had cause to claim on his insurance as a result of some defective act or omission by his self-employed assistant. *Unless specially agreed and arranged, there is no automatic waiver of subrogation against self-employed staff.* So an architect who opts to go 'self-employed' should either take out his own indemnity policy or ensure that the facts of his con-tractual arrangements are declared to his employer's insurers and that they agree to waive their rights of subrogation.

Similarly, in excuse or mitigation of a defect, the self-employed contracted architect cannot plead as effectively as can a salaried architect that his work-ing conditions were bad, that he was obeying instructions, or that he was inadequately supervised. As a self-employed man, he is considered to be a responsible and independent free agent, exercising his professional skill, judge-ment, and ethics at all times.

3.9.2 Agency workers

The position of an 'agency worker' may be a little different, depending on whether he is employed by the agency and simply hired out by it, or maintains his self-employed status and is merely 'placed' by the agency, which takes as its commission a proportion of his earnings. There are so many variants that the best advice is always to establish precisely the relationship of the various parties to the arrangements. If you do not like what you see, then don't stick your neck out.

Although this book is not written for the benefit of proprietors of professional staff agencies, I would add my view that agencies may well carry a legal liability for the technical competence, skill, and care of the staff they hire out. I do not know of a case of an agency being sued or joined in a case for compensation, but I can see no reason why they should be exempt. Most agencies include some kind of exclusion of liability in their trading terms but, depending on circum-stances, these may not be sustainable under the unfair terms legislation.

3.9.3 Ghosting: the unseen perils

Finally, I come to the question of 'ghosting' — the arrangement whereby one architect does all or part of another architect's work, usually on his own premises and generally under the shield of the principal architect's name. These arrangements sometimes masquerade under euphemisms such as 'work-sharing' or 'load-shedding', but they all share the following distinguishing features. The name of the architect actually doing the work is never publicly displayed. And the work is carried out without the direct supervision or control of the principal architect — though he may, of course, subject it to a most minute scrutiny before he actually issues it.

Ghosting is well established in the profession, and a few years ago, in what achieved the proportions of a cause célèbre, an architect was cleared of allegations of professional misconduct which arose when he advertised in the professional press for ghosting assignments. This is a little surprising when one considers that one of the standard terms in the *Architect's appointment* is that no part of an architect's responsibility shall be assigned without the consent in writing of the client. And Note 1.01 in the RIBA Code lays on an architect the responsibility for ensuring that *his* resources are adequate for the task he under-takes, and Rule 1.3 in the Code similarly bars sub-letting of work without the client's written consent.

So first and foremost, if an architect employs a ghost without obtaining the written consent of his client, he is probably in breach of contract, and certainly in breach of the Code of Conduct Rule 1.3. However, widespread though the practice undoubtedly is, there is no recorded case of a member being disciplined for employing ghosts, and I mention the contractual aspects merely en passant. Ghosting takes place at many levels, from a student helping out a one-man band to the wholesale sub-letting of work stages E, F, and G, sometimes C and D, and quite often K, by substantial practices to other (possibly smaller) practices or individuals.

3.9.3.1 Ghosts and material facts

I have no doubt that practitioners who employ ghosts will always say that they take full responsibility for the ghosted work. Well, if they have not obtained their client's consent, there is no way in which they can avoid that responsi-bility. But that may turn out to be no more than glib self-justification, if things go wrong and a claim is made. So far as the principal firm is concerned, insurers may seek to repudiate liability if they have not been advised of the arrangement. It is little use protesting that the gross fees are included in the declared annual turnover — just who does the work, and the conditions under which it is executed, are material facts, and underwriters who sought to repudiate liability or void the policy would be upheld in that action. So make sure that you notify your insurers of your ghosting arrangements, or the strength of the insurance company that you thought to protect you may prove to be as effective as barbed wire against a Chieftain tank.

When you do advise your insurers of subcontracting arrangements, they will almost certainly want to know details of the arrangements — and to have an assurance that the subcontractor or ghost is suitably insured. Can you blame

Ghosting

them? They may even require you to obtain an indemnity from the ghost in respect of claims arising from the ghost's spectral activities. Whether you will be able to obtain one is another thing.

3.9.3.2 *The part-time ghost*

And what of the ghost himself? How can he best cover his own liabilities? We should consider first the young architect, perhaps just qualified, who takes on ghosting as a spare-time activity, purely to supplement his main income. His arrangements are usually informal, seldom committed to paper, and dare I suggest that the payments received may not even be declared for tax? I think it has to be said that, although the practice is widespread, there is probably no way to cover it that makes economic sense, and while he is doing it, the ghost probably operates at risk. His protection rests mainly in the very informality of the arrangement, the element of concealment on both sides, and the fact that he is not worth suing anyway.

But the aim of most ghosts is to go into private practice at some time, and it is prudent when taking out one's first and subsequent professional indemnity cover to obtain retroactive cover in respect of previous ghosting work. The additional premium will be quite small and good value for the peace of mind it may bring.

3.9.3.3 *The established ghost*

Next we consider the case of the practitioner, perhaps struggling to establish himself, who undertakes ghosting work for a larger practice, perhaps as a stop-gap, or even as a fairly regular occurrence. Here there should be no question of informal arrangements — the conditions under which the work is carried out and the extent of responsibility should be clearly set out in an exchange of letters or a formal agreement. I cannot over-emphasise just how important this is for both parties to the arrangement. This aspect has been dealt with more fully under partial service.

Having established the extent of your responsibility, do not neglect to cover your risks by insurance as best you can. The main point to bear in mind here is the inequality of size that usually exists between the principal firm and the ghost. With the inequality of size of firm, consider the size of the project, which may quite possibly be much larger than the ghost will habitually deal with in his direct commissions. You may not be able to afford an indemnity limit high enough to cover the potential risk, but as a very minimum precaution, advise your insurers of the size of the job you are working on and the nature of the arrangements you have. It is unlikely that a ghost will ever be required to pick up a total bill for damages, but even a small proportion could embarrass, if not break, a small practice if its insurers 'walked away' on the grounds of non-disclosure.

Always ensure that the principal firm has advised its insurers of the arrange-ment: if the principal's insurers repudiate, then the risk to the ghost becomes very real indeed. Obtain, if you can, a waiver of subrogation by the principal's insurers. Better still, ghost only for firms who are insured by the same company or underwriters as yourself; then there is no point is subrogation.

Ghosting by one large firm for another is, in the nature of things, probably quite rare. More likely is some sort of formal or loose consortium where the client is fully aware of, and has approved, the arrangements. Consortia and joint ventures are a topic of their own and beyond the scope of this chapter, but many of the considerations of divided responsibility and maintenance of insurance still apply.

I will end as I began, with a reference to the underlying dishonesty of ghosting arrangements. The dishonesty is implicit in the name. A ghost has no substance, can seldom be seen, is never around when you want him, but may return to haunt you at any time in the future. Because of the element of conceal-ment — usually from the client — there is a natural reluctance to commit too much to paper, a readiness to accept handshakes, promises, and undefined risks, where proper documentation would give everybody better protection.

Checklist: Self-employment and ghosting

1   If the self-employment is merely technical, be sure the employers' insurers have waived their rights of subrogation.

2   The self-employed are responsible for their working conditions and have a higher responsibility for their own actions than the directly employed.

3   Self-employed architects should attempt to obtain an indemnity from the 'employer' in respect of direct claims.

4   Agencies *may* have a liability for the technical competence of the staff they supply.

5   A ghost should ensure that the principal firm is covered in respect of his work, and that the insurers have been informed of the arrangements.

6   Practitioners should obtain retroactive cover in respect of previous ghosting assignments.

4: SOMETHING HAS TO CHANGE

4.1 Unsatisfactory law

Thus far, this book has been concerned mainly with advice — advice about how the law affects architects in particular, and on the actions that architects can take in order to minimise and ameliorate the grosser inequities of its application.

If at times I have permitted some extravagances of view or language to creep into the text, it was only because my impatience with the law did not allow me to await this final section.

The thought must have occurred to you many times in reading thus far that the law related to building defects is a mess that provides justice for no one and satisfaction only to the lawyers and experts who have made it their specialised sphere of practice. The operation of the law has become tangled and tortuous, and the settlement of claims expensive and unduly protracted. If an aggrieved party receives compensation at the end of the road, it will seldom represent the full extent of his loss and costs, and there is no certainty that it will be paid — if it is paid at all — by those who were at fault.

No system of law can be perfect in all cases, and similar complaints can at times be levelled at its operation in other types of damage. But in building matters, the criticisms are valid in nearly every case and are seldom levelled with greater justice than at the very leading cases that form the basis of the law.

The Law Lords, giving judgement in *Pirelli* v *Oscar Faber*, expressed their dissatisfaction in forthright terms, and the grapevine has it that as many as 50 per cent of cases pending at the time could be ruled out of remedy because of the Pirelli decision. *Junior Books* v *Veitchi* established that a complainant could sue in tort for simple economic loss; it did not establish that the complainant could actually obtain it. *Anns* v *Merton* placed responsibilities on local authorities and in practice has had the effect of making the public responsible for compensating the owner of a defective building — surely not the intention. In *Eames* v *North London Estates*, the architect was adjudged to be 35–40 per cent liable — but the architect had no money! In another case of which I know, the architect was adjudged to be 1 per cent (!) to blame — but his insurers had to pick up 100 per cent of the damages that were awarded to the claimant. And so it goes on.

I have spent over 30 years in practice, since 1960 as a principal, and in that time I have seen vast changes both in the construction industry and in the law as it applies to buildings. As a principal, I have seen professional indemnity premiums shoot up from sums that were little more than petty cash to amounts that are second only to rent as an overhead cost. I have witnessed a proliferation of administrative procedures, forms, memos, warranties, indemnities, whose sole purpose is precautionary against the onset of future claims. I have had to re-write my partnership deed and my will to ensure that,

147

in my retirement and after my death, my widow will not be reduced to penury. And because I have the same vulnerability as my fellow architects, I have received my small share of threats of action and actual writs. It is probably tempting providence to say that, at the time of writing, my insurers have never had to pay out on a claim against me. But they have certainly incurred thousands of pounds of costs in investigating and defending claims, and my practice has similarly incurred thousands of pounds in costs in time wasted in reproducing and reading documents, writing statements, attending conferences. Perhaps worst of all, the perils of liability — particularly liability to third parties — has soured the professional relationship an architect has with his client. Admitted or not, an architect today puts his client's interest first only at his peril. The state of fear induces a defensiveness into all professional activities and it shows in much of the architecture that is being produced. If problems arise on a job, an architect's endeavours to seek solutions may well be turned against him subsequently.

For the past several years, as a member of the RIBA's practice committee, I have become increasingly involved with the topic of the architect's professional liability. Everything I have seen and heard in that time has led me to the view that there have to be changes in the way we deal with compensation for building defects. For a certainty, there have to be changes in the law, and almost as certainly there have to be changes in our methods of building procurement. There may well have to be changes in the way architecture is practised in the UK, and finally we need to look critically at the way the risks inherent in building are insured. What follow in the succeeding pages are the cases for some suggested changes. Not all will meet with universal approval, and some may be considered quite unacceptable. The acceptance of some will doubtless be conditional on the introduction of others.

As I wrote at the beginning of this book, I am not an expert and I do not profess to have all the answers. But changes there must be if architecture is to survive and the construction industry prosper.

4.2 The anomalous nature of architecture as a profession

'Hard cases make bad law' is a well known maxim in legal circles. You cannot legislate either in favour of or against every conceivable contingency, and any attempt to amend the law of liability to curb its more outlandish results will, I am afraid, leave us with a greater state of uncertainty than we have at present. The Hurst Committee, an ad hoc group established by the UK Inter-Professional Group, produced proposals that unwittingly illustrate this point. Starting from a desire to protect 'the professional man' from excessive claims, it came up with the idea of limiting professional liability to a set amount in return for the compulsory maintenance by all practitioners of indemnity insurance for the limited sum.

Recognising that the condition of veterinary surgeons differs somewhat from that of civil engineers, the committee moved to the concept of 'enabling legislation' whereby each profession could set up its own unique scheme. In this way, the client public would be aware, when they consulted any particular professional, of the limit of the consultant's liability. It was suggested that the limit should be high enough to cover 'a substantial majority of claims'.

They also proposed that no practitioner should be *permitted* to accept liability above the statutory maximum, as that might give him an unfair commercial and competitive advantage and defeat the purpose of the scheme.

Try to apply those principles to our profession and you would have something akin to a camel with four left hind legs. Numerically, a 'substantial majority' of claims are for less than £100,000, and who would dare to suggest that derisory figure as a maximum? It would lead to project insurance by the client becoming the norm — a subject I deal with later. If such a scheme were to be devised for architects, then the only sensible basis would be a limit related to fee income, maximum size of project, or some other fluctuating figure. So the client — and, more particularly, remote tort sufferers — would never have any idea of the limit of liability on any particular building. The concept of certainty mentioned in 4.1 would have disappeared. There would be other problems as well, but I quote this particular instance to demonstrate just one difficulty with dealing with the professional liabilities of architects. There are others.

Since I first became involved with liability, I have become increasingly aware that the architectural profession fits no common pattern and that only occasionally does it exhibit any similarity with any other profession. It is, in my view, the anomalous nature of the profession and the building process that is at the root of our liability problems. The presumption that architects' liability could be dealt with under the umbrella of generic legislation is ill-conceived and misplaced. Until this is widely understood, any attempts at the amelioration of our condition are likely to make things worse rather than better.

First and foremost, architecture does not have an academic base. Even though it is studied in universities, the educational base is primarily practical and from outside the universities. As evidence of this, I would cite the relative absence of academic research fellowships. The education of an architect is not primarily concerned with the instillation of academic expertise and knowledge, but with the development of thought-processes. For a certainty, the academic and technical knowledge absorbed by the architectural student is not intended to qualify him as an expert in anything.

Architects, if they specialise at all, specialise in being generalists. One does not need to be an experienced jurist to recognise the inanity of expecting in one man the expertise embodied in perhaps 15 degree courses. So, almost alone among the professions, architects are *not* experts.

The effects of the architect's endeavours spread far beyond his immediate commissioning client. When a doctor treats a patient, cause and effect are immediately apparent and only those two parties are concerned. Similarly, with few exceptions, this applies to accountants, lawyers, vets, patent agents — indeed, any profession outside the construction industry.

Just for the exercise, it is as well to list the categories of people who may be affected by the architect's work: his client; mortgagees; subsequent purchasers, lessees, occupants and users; contractors; subcontractors; passers-by.

Again, with many professions, the damage arising from incompetence or negligence is usually soon apparent — sometimes, as with death during surgery, dramatically so. With the construction professions, the damage may be latent for many years, and commonly is. Even after the damage occurs, it may not be perceived, as was so clearly demonstrated in the case of Pirelli's 160ft. high chimney. Take now the question of blame. If a lawyer drafts a defective title, the finger of blame can point unwaveringly at a certain target, as it will at the surgeon whose knife slips. If a building slides unevenly into the surrounding terrain, you *may*, with the fingers of one hand well spread, indicate possible perpetrators of the defect. One of those digits will for a certainty be pointed at the architect — but with what justice, only a long process of investigation may determine.

They may not figure in any writ for damages, but we as architects know that the people, parties, or firms who may have some part of the responsibility for an eventual building defect or failure form an almost endless list. For a certainty, there is a commissioning client, who by the very nature of his requirements (particularly in relation to cost), may at the commencement of the project or later have sown the seeds of ultimate disaster. There is the engineer who carried out the subsoil investigation and may have failed to notice that trees had been removed from the land, creating the conditions for future ground-heave. There is the architect himself, and all his fellow consultants whose work he is expected to understand and integrate or incorporate in his master design. There is the builder, who may be a working governor with half a dozen tradesmen or a vast corporation carrying out hundreds of millions of pounds' worth of construction each year. Given that size alone is no guarantee of appropriate site or workplace skills, the scope for failure here is enormous. Then there are all the miscellaneous and specialist subcontractors working under independent supervision in a wide range of technologies. There are the component manufacturers and the makers and suppliers of materials, many of which are in a constant and continuous process of change and development.

It is in bringing together the skills of all these people and the properties of all the components and materials that the architect exercises his own skills in order to create a completed building. There is probably no artefact in our society as complex in its procurement as a building. And when it is finally assembled, it is subjected to the use and abuse of an occupant who may understand nothing of the processes and materials incorporated in his building and who may fail to inspect and maintain it in a proper fashion.

In the creation of a building, the architect's role very largely consists of making a series of value judgements. He has to balance the requirements of the client's brief against utility, visual delight, first cost, durability and cost in use, and so on. His task is not finite, nor is it capable of being judged in a finite manner. Furthermore, each building is, in essence, a prototype. In bringing together a multitude of materials and components, there is no possibility of testing the completed product other than by observing it in use after completion. Each decision which involves the making of value judgements opens an area of risk, particularly the risk of hindsight. The same applies to some extent to many of the other parties involved in the construction process, but for most of them there are routes which can be followed which lessen their exposure to the risks.

In the end, it is the architect who carries the burden, at least in part, for all the risks inherent in the construction process. In my view, this is not only unreasonable, but it makes no sense. Society requires buildings, and creating buildings — particularly in an age of developing technology and rising public expectation — is a hazardous operation. In my view, it is right and proper that society, for whose benefit buildings are created, should accept as its own burden the risks and hazards inherent in building. It is, in any event, becoming increasingly evident that individual building designers are not able to carry that burden of risk through insurance. Where there have been cases of major failure of public buildings (and for that matter, private buildings as well), the ability of an owner to recoup his losses through his rights at law has been shown to be severely limited.

Finally, it is worth contemplating the relationship between the design cost of a building and the cost of the article itself. In round terms, for most buildings, the fees of the design team — that is, architect, structural consultant, and M&E engineers — is in the order of 10 per cent of the cost of the final product. (I have excluded the cost of the quantity surveyor because his primary function has little or nothing to do with the design, and the major part of his fees is related to the competitive-tender process and the adversarial nature of the standard construction contracts.) This 10 per cent of the cost of the product should be compared with the design input that goes into all the other artefacts created by our society. Even allowing for the difference in unit cost between the building and the dry shaver or the motorcar, it takes but a moment's contemplation to convince one of the disparity of resource allocated to the design (and supervision of construction) of buildings and the resource allocated to the design and development of other manufactured products. The cost of developing a motorcar with a unit cost of £5,000 may be as much as 1000 times the unit cost, and still windscreens leak, bodywork rusts, tyres burst, and the vehicle itself may be consigned to the scrapyard after five or six years, or alternatively last for 20 years or more. With prototypes and production models tested to destruction, manufacturers still have to recall from use entire production runs of models in order to replace some patently defective component. If this is the outcome of such a massive design effort as is put into the motorcar, to what extent should the failure of a building ever be attributed to the negligence of the designers?

I return to my contention that the practice of architecture is anomalous among the professions. Performance cannot be judged by the standards applied to other professions, nor can responsibility be allocated in a similar way. By its very nature, architecture is an imperfect profession to be practised with care, but with an acknowledgement that there will always be a risk of failure in the ultimate product.

The remuneration of the architect may bear some relation to the cost of the product, but it bears no relation whatsoever to the potential size of the ultimate risk and responsibility he bears, given the present state of the law. And there is a counter-productivity inherent in the system, because the greater the care the architect takes, both to protect his client and to protect himself, the lower in real terms becomes the remuneration of the profession. As remuneration is driven down (and the latest earnings survey by the RIBA shows a very

serious relative erosion over the past 10 years), then the lower will be the calibre
of entrants into the profession, and there will be a downward spiral of talent,
competence, and dedication. This is a matter which can only cause the gravest
concern at a time when the skills required in the profession are constantly
becoming more complex. Widespread recognition of this phenomenon is
necessary in the interests of both the profession and the construction industry.
The submission made by the Royal Institute of British Architects to the Law
Reform Committee's sub-committee on latent defects made the point very
strongly that, where the construction industry was concerned, the problems of
inequity and certainty would not be dealt with by tinkering with the existing
generic law. The case was made strongly that the peculiar and special features
of the construction process required specific legislation if they were to be
resolved satisfactorily.

4.3 Changes in the law

Elsewhere in this book, I have sought to show that the application of the law of
the land to the problems created by defects in buildings just does not work.
The principles of fairness on which the law is founded are ill-served by a process
which only too often penalises innocent parties and fails to compensate those
who have suffered injury. Too often it is only the interests of the lawyers and the
professional expert witnesses that are served by the attempt to apply our traditional generic laws of contract and tort to the highly complex problems of
responsibility that are inherent in the building process. We are rapidly
approaching a situation which will bring the law itself into disrepute and make
it a laughing-stock.

At the time of writing this book, there is one case going the rounds where the
biggest problem has been to find a place large enough to accommodate the two
dozen warring parties, their leading counsel, their junior counsel, their
solicitors, and their experts. With the case liable to run in court for over a year,
it has been necessary to lease a complete floor of one of the large London clubs
in order that justice shall be done; and it is estimated that the cost of obtaining
that justice will run into several millions of pounds. I know neither the facts of
the case nor the amount of money involved, although clearly it is substantial,
but it is unlikely that a war of attrition on this scale will result in anything but
a pyrrhic victory for any of the contestants. I am presuming that each of the
contestants is, in fact, covered by an insurer, and what we are really down to is
an adjudication on how the risk should be picked up within the insurance
market.

At the other end of the scale, there are cases of ex-practitioners of great age
and in poor heath who have been hounded in their retirement for professional
acts, or omissions, performed up to 30 years previously. Commonly there are
cases where claimants with absolutely justified complaints receive no
compensation, simply because the responsible party no longer exists or has
neither the wealth nor the insurance to make restitution. There are cases
where defendants with only a minor responsibility find themselves with the
liability to pay the whole of the cost of damages. The catalogue of inequities and
iniquities inherent in the law relating to building defects is endless, and the

time is long overdue for some lateral thinking on the subject.

We must start from the premise that there will always be building failures. By its very nature, any building is a unique creation, however similar it may be to its neighbour. Buildings are made by hand, often under appalling conditions of weather, and are situated on the natural element of the earth, the behaviour of which cannot be accurately predicted. After completion, each building is used in a unique manner internally and subjected externally to the unpredictable ravages of the climate. Each unique building has a very high unit value, and its failure can result in catastrophic losses to its owner or occupant. Finally, it is constructed of components, each with differing durability, and in total has no defined period of effective life. Yet, in essence, it is subjected to the same expectations as the factory–built product covered under the Sale of Goods Act. Notwithstanding the banner headlines drawing attention to building failures, the simple fact is that we have an extremely low failure rate in modern buildings and one which compares very favourably with almost any other modern industrialised nation.

It is inevitable, however, that some buildings sooner or later will fail. To attempt to create a situation where all buildings would be failure-proof for all time is a fruitless task. It could only be achieved at a cost to society far greater than society would be prepared to accept. Civilised man accepts a level of risk in everything he does. There is a risk in getting out of bed in the morning and, for that matter, a risk in turning over and going back to sleep. Given the risk, the law should address itself to dealing in a sensible manner with those cases where the risk is realised and eventuates in a building failure. The law should be based on two principles: certainty and equity.

The principle of certainty is of prime significance. With the law in its present state, there is no certainty that a damaged party will be compensated at all, or that he will be compensated in the right amount, or, most particularly, that he will be compensated at the right time. For those engaged in the construction industry, there is no certainty that they will ever be free of their liability, or of the sum in which that liability may eventually come home to roost.

English law professes to hold the balance of fairness between the parties. Much of the law in respect of building defects has been based on failure of domestic properties. There is no greater disaster for the average man than to lose the house which he has mortgaged a large part of his lifetime earnings to acquire. The sympathy of the courts is manifest, particularly when the claim in the first instance is directed against a large building corporation. Too often this is an illusion on a par with the three-card trick or sawing a lady in half. For it is not the householder who has lost his all, but the mega-million pound insurance company seeking to recoup compensation it has already paid out, and for which it had previously accepted the houseowner's premiums. And, more often than not, it will not be the building corporation, which went into liquidation long since, but a professional practitioner, maybe even an ex-professional practitioner, who may have earned very little indeed for the service for which he is now being held responsible in an amount which may be several thousand times his original fee. The Law Reform Committee's sub-committee on latent defects in its consultative document recognised the need to hold a balance of fairness in building-defects cases, and it remains to be seen how far its recommendations will go to meet this need.

There is nothing new in the concept of specific legislation. We already have the Defective Premises Act, which applies to houses, and we have a three-year period of limitation in cases of personal injury. If we are to have specific legislation, however, it needs to be comprehensive and not simply dealing with the period of limitation and accrual of cause. How should we go about this? In the following pages, I propose some ways in which the law could be developed to meet the needs of the producers and users of buildings.

4.3.1 Certainty in time

Without any doubt at all, the priority is to achieve some certainty in time. Lord Scarman was rightly critical of the law when, several years after the commencement of litigation, he had to adjudicate that Pirelli were time-barred against Oscar Faber. Whether the decision was right or wrong is beside the point. What is quite outrageous is that Pirelli, who thought they had a perfectly good claim, had to go through the three layers of our judicial process to find that they were time-barred from the outset, and accordingly were left without remedy.

In its submission to the Law Reform Committee, the RIBA proposed that no claim should be made in respect of building defects more than six years after the date of practical completion of a building. To cover the case of an architect who was employed on partial service only and may have had no part in the building process itself, there was a further longstop limit of 10 years from the latest date at which the architect had an involvement. Other professionals involved in the construction industry similarly proposed definite time limitations, some dating from the negligent act, some from the completion of the building.

Subsequently, the RIBA commissioned the drafting of a bill, the intention of which is to set a time limit of 10 years from the date of completion for the bringing of any claims arising from defects in a building. The exercise was carried out primarily to demonstrate the practicality of such legislation, and it was recognised that it would stand little or no chance of being enacted as a private member's bill. It has been submitted to the Law Reform Committee as a general aid to their deliberations, and to the Secretary of State for the Environment, with a request for urgent action.

In the discussions which took place in the formulation of this bill, it was noticeable that there was quite a wide gulf between the architects and the lawyers involved. The lawyers found great difficulty in accepting a limitation period based on anything other than either the original defective act or omission, or a date, related to the damage itself. They felt that the date of completion of the building was irrelevant to the legal basis of a claim, and it was only with considerable reluctance that they accepted the architects' view that the concept of certainty was more important than a hypothetical legal principle. The view of the architects promoting the bill was that it was possible to define, at the time, the date of completion of the building, and therefore both the building owner and the potential defendants in any claim would know exactly where

they stood and the date on which their rights or responsibilities expired.
It is interesting to note that within the course of one year, the RIBA proposed
two different time limits to the Law Reform Commission — six years and 10
years. This is not particularly indicative of any confusion or difference of
opinion within the institute as to what might be the correct period. If the
choice were up to me, I would select six years, which ties up with the period
written into the Defective Premises Act. Certainly, the vast majority of defects
in buildings appear within a six-year period after completion, and if a building
has stood and functioned properly for that period, there should be little difficulty for the building owner in insuring the subsequent risk of failure for a very
modest premium indeed. The attraction of 10 years is the existence of an
insurance market prepared to underwrite that period, and it is also the period
much in use within the Common Market. It has the merit that, in the eyes of
most people, it is so excessive a period that the building designers and constructors are clearly not trying to evade or avoid any proper responsibility, and
to that extent it probably has a greater chance of finding its way to the statute
book.
Whichever period is adopted is really of little consequence. Of major importance is the establishment of a set period of which everybody will be aware. In
principle, it makes little difference whether the period is one year, six years, or
10 years; the important thing is that there shall be a firm date before which the
building creators have a liability, and beyond which the liability falls upon the
building owner. Only with that kind of certainty in law is it possible to deal with
the problems arising from building defects in a satisfactory manner.

4.3.2 Certainty in amount
Earlier in this book, I attempted to describe the difficulty an architect has in
deciding the limit of professional indemnity cover that he should purchase. As
the law stands at present, his liability is as long as the metaphorical piece of
string. While an intelligent guess can be made at the effects of inflation, it is
simply not possible for an architect, or anybody else involved in the building
procurement process, to do more than conjecture what the consequential
losses might be in the event of a building failure. I have referred to the comparatively minor case of *Junior Books* v *Veitchi*, where the 'economic loss'
amounted to three times the cost of making good the physical damage. The case
was fairly typical, but the ratio of 3:1 could just as easily have been 10:1, or even
greater. Again I will reiterate that the right to compensation may be quite
illusory if the defendant does not have the resources to meet it, and the ability to
sue for consequential loss creates uncertainty for both defendant and claimant.
The only party in a position to know the extent of the consequential losses
arising from a building failure is the building owner and/or occupant himself. It
is an insurable risk, covered in respect of all other building hazards such as fire
and flood, and there is absolutely no reason why it should not be similarly
covered in respect of building defects or failures.
It has long been possible for an architect to exclude his liability for of consequential loss in his contract with his client. Although not many architects took
advantage of their ability to do so, the principle was clearly accepted and the

good sense and fairness of the principle could not be denied. Since the enact-
ment of the unfair contract terms legislation, the RIBA has advised its members
that any limitation of liability for consequential loss might possibly be dis-
allowed as an unfair term. So far, this has not been put to the test, although I
would suggest that the converse applies, and the more common situation —
where the architect, for one sixteenth of the cost of the product, may be liable for
damages many times the value of the product — is a grossly unfair contract
term in itself, and dates back to the Victorian concept of liability 'down to his
cufflinks'. While I would not go so far as to suggest that limitation in amount
should be related to the fee, in the way that dry-cleaners only accept liability up
to 40 times the cost of cleaning, nevertheless some limitation there must be if we
are to have certainty of compensation.

It was the judicial decision that the building owner could sue in tort if he
wished, rather than rely on his contract, together with the decision in Junior
Books, which undermined the very sensible procedure of limiting one's contractual liability. In extending the rights of claimants in this way, the law has
merely created a large area of uncertainty, and it is time for new legislation to
put the matter right. We require legislation which limits the liability of the
parties concerned in the creation of buildings to the cost of remedying the
physical damage.

If certainty of compensation of a damaged party is the objective of the law, the
only figure that can be determined with some accuracy at the time of the completion of a building project is the cost of the building at that time. It seems to
be no more than common sense that that figure should be the limit of the building provider's liability. Provisions for inflation are always very difficult to
legislate for, but if that were the wish of the public at large and the legislators,
I have no doubt that it could be dealt with in a way that was still capable of
being covered by the building provider's insurances.

4.3.3 Compulsory insurance

The criticism is always made of the professions that, while they claim to accept
responsibility for their actions 'down to their cufflinks', the claim is quite
spurious because they may have no assets to back up their liability. It is a fact
that most architects do carry insurance, although the limit of the indemnity that
is covered may, in some cases, be less than might be thought to be desirable.
In the recent survey carried out by the RIBA, it was only among the very
smallest practices that a significant proportion of practitioners was uninsured, and even among the one-man firms, the uninsured proportion was
less than a quarter. Among the two-man firms, that proportion had dropped to
five per cent, and above that size, virtually all firms did purchase professional
indemnity cover.

So the need for insurance is clearly recognised by the profession, and that
recognition is largely translated into action. The reasons why so many lone
practitioners do not carry insurance are not known, but it may have quite a bit
to do with their difficulty in continuing their insurance through periods of low
income and after retirement. It is not unreasonable to take the view that, if you
cannot cover yourself properly, there may be little point in covering yourself at

all. A further reason may be the belief that the mere possession of insurance cover invites claims, and for the lone practitioner who has only himself to consider, 'going bare' may be considered a legitimate form of protection. Pressure is, however, mounting from a number of directions for it to be made obligatory for professionals of all kinds to carry suitable and adequate insurance if they offer their services to the public. Solicitors have for some years had a compulsory scheme enforced through the Law Society, and most recently the chartered surveyors have instituted a similar scheme. The possibility of instituting a requirement to insure has been debated at intervals by the RIBA, most recently at the time when it was revising the Code of Conduct to permit firms to practise in the form of limited liability companies. On that occasion, the proposal to compel those practices that opted for the change of form to carry insurance was defeated on the grounds that it was discriminatory, although the whole tenor of the debate was clearly in favour of compulsory insurance generally.

In giving its qualified approval to the proposals of the Hurst Committee (referred to above), the RIBA was clearly prepared to accept the principle of compulsory insurance, and if a satisfactory scheme could be arranged, I have little doubt that it would be adopted.

Any system of compulsory insurance brings in its train a number of subsidiary measures because, obligation or not, there will always be occasions when the statutory or other obligation has not been complied with. One of the problems which will undoubtedly arise in the construction-design professions is the variation in terms between one underwriter and another. Any system of compulsory insurance would require the laying down of standard wording to comply with the law. This may prove to be easier said than done, although it was achieved in the most common of compulsory insurances — that related to motor vehicles.

Similarly, as with compulsory motor insurance, a compensation fund would have to be established to take care of those cases where, for some reason or other, no valid insurance was in force. The simplest way of organising a system of compulsory insurance is through a single underwritten scheme. There are both advantages and objections to such schemes from both sides of the contract, in that the insured, having no choice, considers himself held to ransom by the insurers, and the insurers have to give up their rights to choice of 'risk'.

Given an open market, there might still arise the problem of the firm which, for some reason or other, might be unable to obtain insurance at any price. While this might only happen exceptionally it could be quite catastrophic for an established firm that suddenly found itself unable to practise. Herein is perhaps the greatest objection to compulsory insurance, and how to deal with it is a matter which will need considerable thought.

Compulsory insurance of design professionals is well established in other countries, and it is usually effected through a centralised scheme administered jointly by the insurers and the professional institute involved. There are very substantial advantages to this type of arrangement. Not least is the knowledge which becomes available to the profession about the nature and causes of claims, and the feedback that the professional institute can give to its members

on steps they can take to reduce the likelihood of building failures. Faced with
what almost amounts to a conspiracy of silence under the present system in
this country, the RIBA has been able to do very little along these lines. We are
rapidly moving into an era where professional institutes are expected by the
public to monitor the performance of their members and to assist them in
maintaining and improving their competence. For that reason alone, I feel it is
inevitable that some sort of centralised monitored scheme will sooner or later be
adopted.

If the objective of compulsory insurance is certainty of compensation for injured
parties, then quite clearly there has to be a defined and finite risk that has to be
insured. Given some reasonable time–limit on liability and a clear method of
defining the sum that shall be insured, the profession would be ready to accept
an obligation to insure imposed by its institute, by the registration council, or
by statute. It might even be prepared to accept an obligation from the institute
without changes in the law, but most of the uncertainties in the present system
would remain, and the primary objective would not have been achieved.

If insurance were to be made obligatory in the interest of certainty, then the
standard professional indemnity policy as we know it will need drastic
revision, and the form it should take is dealt with below.

4.3.4 The judicial concept of negligence

Both in contract and in tort, an architect's liability stems from the judicial concept of negligence. It is the need to prove or disprove negligence that creates
much of the uncertainty, dissatisfaction, and cost in building-failure claims.
Given that nobody is deliberately negligent, proof of 'lack of care' can only be
deduced, and in the courts that deduction is made on a basis of expert
evidence and hindsight. In fact, whatever may be said in defence of the present
system, the basis of most findings of negligence in building cases is a simple
failure to 'get it right'.

The determination of blame through the judicial process has become more and
more difficult with the increasing complexity of buildings, and even with the
benefit of hindsight, many of the findings of negligence do not even match up
to Solomon's proposal that baby be chopped in half.

When the courts are further required to apportion the contributory negligence
of the multifarious participants in the construction process, then the difficulty of
making relevant and reasoned decisions becomes clear. Architects particularly
resent the responsibility they are adjudged to bear for the builder's failure to
build properly, as do the local authorities in respect of the builder's failure
(sometimes deliberate) to comply with the regulations.

If we are to have judicial assessment of negligence, then I would propose the
concept of 'primary responsibility': designers to be responsible for the correct-
ness of their design, builders to be responsible for building in accordance with
the design, and manufacturers and suppliers to take responsibility if the failure
is due to their products.

This may be venturing into the realms of absolute product liability, but it would
certainly be more just than the present system, where the overlapping
responsibilities lead to a tangled skein of litigation from which nobody

benefits. And I believe that it would mean a reversion to a definition of negligence which is much closer to the true meaning of the word than a mere failure to be perfect. The onus of proof of negligence should be on the claimant. It should not be sufficient merely to deduce from a defect that negligence had been committed.

I have a letter on file from the wife of an aged and ailing practitioner who is being sued by an ecclesiastical authority over some rising damp in an old church in which he had been involved in some underpinning: 'I know the care, and dare I say love, that he put into this church . . .' I believe her, but her husband is being accused — and, if it goes to court, will probably be adjudged guilty — of negligence. The church is, of course, advised by lawyers.

It has been put to me that if the creators of buildings were relieved of their responsibility not to be negligent, then this would encourage them to be less careful than they are at the present in the knowledge of the burden they carry. One cannot deny that this might happen, although I do not believe that a lowering of standards would be widespread. Indeed, there is a better-than-even chance that standards of professional endeavour might actually rise as, relieved of the need to protect their rear at every turn, building designers could actually concentrate on designing better buildings. It might be that all those value judgements the architect has to make could be made on a true appraisal of all the relevant factors, without the intrusion of his own personal interest.

What options are open to us to deal with the deliberately negligent, reckless, or incompetent professional practitioner? Increasingly, the public view is that the professional institutes should monitor and discipline the performance of their members. There are those who would not be satisfied by that sort of internal arrangement, but would demand some kind of statutory control of licences to practise. Certainly, it is unlikely that the right to call oneself a member of a profession and to practise that profession will for much longer depend solely on entry qualifications.

The official view in the RIBA, when complaints have been levelled at its members by members of the public, is that negligence or incompetence are a matter for the courts. We can see the sort of mess the courts make of dealing with this most vexed problem, and, in my view, there is greater scope for misjudgement when these matters are being assessed by lawyers and others not intimately concerned with the building process than if they are dealt with by the offender's co-professionals. One of the arguments always put up against the RIBA's disciplining its members for negligence or professional incompetence is that, by so doing, the institute could prejudice a case which might be running a parallel course in the courts. If the adjudication of negligence or incompetence were taken away from the ambit of the courts, then this major objection would no longer apply.

If the right to practise depended on continuing membership of a professional institute, or on some form of statutory registration that could be taken away following a finding of negligent or incompetent practice, then there would certainly have to be safeguards that such a grave penalty was not imposed lightly. Most failures to reach an expected standard of competence or service arise not from deliberate neglect but simply because the sheer complexity of the process is beyond the resources of the practitioner concerned. Cases like these can be dealt with by means of reprimand, inspection, and probation, and I would envisage the withdrawal of a licence to practise or of membership of an institute as a penalty to be imposed only in the gravest of cases, or on persistent refusal to mend one's ways.

To me, the issue is a simple one. The ability to practise under the umbrella of the corporate reputation of a professional institute is an extremely valuable privilege. The institute has an absolute right to maintain its image and the reputation of its members by insisting on the maintenance of standards of practice by all its members, and I can think of few who would contest that view. It is my firm belief that, if matters of negligence and competence were taken out of the realms of the courts, then the institutes, or registration councils, or whatever, could find quite adequate and satisfactory sanctions to ensure that any sort of legal immunity was not abused.

4.4 Changes in insurance

4.4.1 Decennial professional liability insurance

Even today, when there has been so much publicity on the subject of professional indemnity insurance and building claims, there are architects who are surprised to discover, when a claim arises, that they have no insurance cover. They may have been in practice some years previously, but having given up practice to retire or to take salaried employment, they have let their policies lapse. When a legal assault is made on them in respect of some long-finished project, they contact the insurers to whom they paid their premiums when they were carrying out the works. The insurance company, not surprisingly, expresses supreme uninterest, and the architect is left to ruminate on the injustice of it all.

Not a few of the problems faced by practitioners derive from the annual basis on which the standard professional indemnity insurance policy is written. It occurs to me that if only we could achieve a statutory time-limit for liability of (say) 10 years, then the way would be open for rewriting the standard professional indemnity policy on an entirely different basis. Just as it is possible even now for a building owner to purchase decennial insurance for a building he has commissioned, so there is no reason why an architect should not purchase insurance running for 10 years and covering all those projects which, within the year of the policy, had achieved practical completion. The premium would probably be paid by way of a deposit at the commencement of the year, based on the size and turnover of the practice and adjusted at the end by reference to the completions achieved during the insurance period. The immediate and evident advantage of such a policy is that the premiums would be paid in respect of projects out of the fees for them at the time they accrued. At a stroke, this would do away with the problems of run-off insurance on retirement and reduced income during periods of fluctuating workflow.

An objection one might anticipate from the insurance industry is that insurers do their accounting on a rolling three-year term, and there might be difficulty in finding a sufficient body of underwriters prepared to keep their accounts open for 10 years. In the light of experience with building defects, there would in effect be little change from what happens at the present time. What happens with the annual contract is that, before the accounts are closed at the end of three years, reserves are set against all those matters of which they have been notified and are still not settled. As it is by no means uncommon for notifications to remain open for 10 years before settlement, and the underwriters retain their liability regardless of the size of the reserve they have written in, the closing of the accounts is no more than an administrative and accountancy exercise. Changing over to a 10-year period would seem to present very little difficulty in practice.

One other advantage that would derive from this form of project-related insurance is the solution of the dilemma faced by part-time or occasional practitioners. Traditionally, one of the ways of commencing a practice is by carrying on a part-time practice while in salaried employment. A single commission may be the springboard from which a young architect will go on to establish a full-time practice, or it may not. If it is the only job he ever does and he wishes to maintain his insurance cover on it under the present system, then in the long term his premiums may well exceeed the fee he has received. In practical terms, part-time and occasional practice is uninsurable and uninsured. Given a form of project-related insurance, this gap in insurance protection would be easy to fill. Insofar as most part-time and occasional practitioners are working for domestic and small industrial clients, the need for insurance is perhaps even more crucial than in other areas.

So here is something for the insurance industry to ponder. All professional indemnity policies had their origin in what old-timers referred to as 'errors and omissions' insurance. As the variation in the risks between one profession and another has become evident, so specific policies have been developed for each, but the basis has remained the same. Where the building industry and the construction professions are concerned, the time has come for a complete re-think.

Such a policy would probably need to be written in two parts, so that claims arising from contemporary activities and claims arising before completion of a building would also be covered, but I am quite certain that it is not beyond the wit of policy draughtsmen to devise a document which would be much more useful and relevant than the present one. If, by statute, an architect's liability was limited to the cost of making good physical damage, there would be no difficulty in indexing the insured sum to the cost of construction, and this could be taken into account in the initial premium. This is, in fact, even easier to deal with than it might appear, because premium funds are invested at interest rates which reflect the rate of inflation, and the greater the length of time that elapses before the claim, the larger the premium fund becomes.

However, all this is something for the future, because it depends entirely upon the law being altered in the ways I have already indicated.

4.4.2 Comprehensive project insurance
Much of what has gone before served to demonstrate the shortcomings of our existing arrangements for insurance. What was originally devised as a protec-

tion for the professional practitioner and a safeguard for his client in fairly exceptional circumstances has in recent years turned into something rather different, and something for which it is by its very nature ill-suited. Just as a house-purchaser will look on his survey report as a lifetime guarantee, so the building owner or occupier today tends to look upon the insurance cover of his professionals as an insurance of the building itself. The courts have supported that view, with the result that professional indemnity underwriters are called on with increasing frequency to incur massive defence costs and pay out ever-increasing sums. Insurers who have been long in the field have decided to withdraw, and while there is no shortage of newcomers prepared to pick up their mantle, the market is restricted, premiums are constantly rising, and practitioners are finding it more and more difficult to obtain insurance cover in the sums they need and at a cost in premiums that they can afford.

Some while ago, I wrote an article pointing out some of the difficulties and some of the evasive tactics that an architect could adopt. When it was published, I received a telephone call from a solicitor specialising in professional indemnity defences, in which he congratulated me on the article, which he had found very interesting. But he went on to say, 'You've missed the main point. The real problem is that your fees are not high enough'. My subsequent conversations with this solicitor have convinced him that even increasing fees would not enable architects to deal with many of the problems which arise from their professional liability. At the same time, I have come to the view that the fee-scales promulgated by the RIBA, particularly for works up to £1m, are simply an inadequate return for the service the architect is, in the eyes of the law, required to give. That, however, is another issue, perhaps to be argued in another place.

A form of insurance which answers most of the needs of the building owner has been common on the Continent for many years, and has been used for some isolated projects in this country. It goes under various names, but in essence, it is the building that is insured against defects for a set period of years on payment of a single premium at the outset.

Project insurance was primarily devised for the protection of the building owner, and in its currently marketed form, it has little to commend it to building designers or constructors. Indeed, in some respects, it may make their plight even worse. But there seems to be no reason why, given a sufficiently large market, project insurance could not be written in such a manner as to provide protection to all the parties to a building contract, and the cost would fairly represent the hazards inherent in all kinds of building projects.

Project insurance works in the following way.

The insured (i.e., the building owner) arranges his insurance before construction of the building starts. He pays a proportion of the premiums as a deposit, and when he takes possession of the building — that is, at practical completion — the balance of the premium is payable, and the cover for a set period, usually 10 years, begins to run. The risks covered in the insurance are basically collapse and settlement, but they may also include water penetration and other defects. At least one policy currently available covers all inherent and latent building defects of a substantial nature. Certain risks, such as water penetration, do not come under cover until the expiration of the defects liability period. The amount of cover is the estimated cost of reconstructing the building, and it is possible to make arrangements for indexing this at the commencement, or for increasing it year by year on payment of an additional premium.

The insurers naturally wish to be reasonably certain that they are not insuring a project with foreseeable defects, and their acceptance of the insurance is conditional upon their own experts inspecting the plans, specifications, and so on, and making inspections of the construction as it proceeds. It is possible, for an increased premium, to arrange for the insurers to waive their rights of subrogation against the design team. At the present time, there are no arrangements for them to waive their rights of subrogation against the builder, or any other subcontractors, materials or component suppliers, and the like.

With project insurance as it is currently written, and with the law as it stands, there are a number of very real drawbacks for the design team. Perhaps the biggest danger, so far as architects are concerned, is the fear that the insurers will not be prepared to cover any innovative features in a design because of the greater risk inherent in them. The inspectorate employed or appointed by the insurers has only one interest to consider, that of the underwriters themselves, and inevitably they have no carefully balanced judgements to make. If they think that any feature represents an enhanced risk, then regardless of the other benefits which might flow from that feature, there is a fear that they will veto it. In the extreme, we could find ourselves in a position where the insurers are dictating the design of buildings solely in the interest of the preservation of their premium fund.

The second objection, which is very important to practising professionals, is the effective loss of the confidentiality of their own failure records. One of the great advantages of the professional indemnity insurance system is that one's lapses remain known only to the client, oneself, and one's insurers. Granted that you may pay a much heavier premium as a result of successful claims against you, but at least your public reputation is not jeopardised. With project insurance, it is possible that this would no longer apply, and it does not take too fertile an imagination to conceive that a building owner might seek premium quotes for a project on the basis of two different design teams. If a member of one of those design teams had a bad record, then different premiums might be quoted. In that case, an unfortunate architect would not just be paying an enhanced premium, he would be in danger of losing commissions. In discussions I have had with insurers, I have been assured that the market would be wide enough for this not to happen, and one would hope that this would be so — but the doubt remains.

However, even with the insurers waiving their rights of subrogation against the design team, neither the architect nor the insurers could be free of the cost of litigation. If, for instance, the insurers decided to exercise their rights against the builder, there would be no impediment to his joining in for contribution all or any members of the design team. Even were the insurers under the policy to indemnify the design team against this contingency, we would still be left with the tangled process of deciding and allocating proportions of blame.

I have discussed with insurers the possibility of writing a form of policy of building-guarantee insurance, in which all rights of subrogation were waived. Such a policy could probably be written, 'but the cost would be prohibitive'. My feeling about that comment is that it may be no more than a conditioned reflex by the insurers. On closer examination they might discover that since they would not have to mount either aggressive or defensive litigation, the savings might go some considerable way towards counteracting the increased risk. Certainly, over the insurance market as a whole, there would be gains if there is any truth at all in the stories one hears of insurers paying out £1 in legal and defence costs for every £1 of damage claim.

The fears that project insurance would result in the dead hand of defensive design being laid across the design process need to be allayed. A form of policy I have discussed with one insurer would leave the choice of the inspecting agency up to the insured, and this would seem to meet the major objections. What is envisaged is a wide panel of approved inspecting agencies, among which the insured, or his design team, would have complete freedom of choice. It would be possible to select as an inspecting agency a firm with a similar design philosophy to one's own. The costs of employing the inspecting agency, in any event, fall on the insured under this type of policy, so one might find oneself paying for the privilege of selection, but at least there would be established a working relationship of collaboration rather than one of opposition.

The idea of an inspecting agency seems to fit in very well with the current legislation on private certification of buildings for compliance with Building Regulations. It is no mere coincidence that the consultation paper the Department of the Environment put out on this issue floated the idea of project insurance quite strongly, and also coincidentally, and by implication, the idea of time limitation. Perhaps the most difficult problem to solve on project guarantee insurance is, 'who pays?'. One can understand the disinclination of the building owner to bear the whole of the cost when, in effect, he is insuring the activities of the other parties to the building procurement process. It is estimated that building-guarantee insurance written on a totally non-recourse basis, and for a 10-year period, might cost as much as 2 per cent of the insured sum. That is many times the cost of professional indemnity insurance, at present borne by the design team, and clearly it could not be found from within design fees at the existing level. In fact, however the premiums are split up between the various parties receiving the protection of the policy, the cost of this protection is part of the cost of the building and will have to be found by the building owner. I subscribe to the view that he will receive good value for the premium, not only in the protection it provides, but also in the better building that will result from it.

4.5 Changes in the practice of architecture

In a sense, many of the problems of liability from which the profession of architecture suffers at the present time have been brought upon us by the way in which we practise our profession. In an era of rapidly changing technology and increasing specialisation, only architects insist on claiming an omniscience and ubiquity that cannot be sustained. As leaders of the building team, our fingers are in every part of the building pie, and it could be that we are simply paying the penalty for greed and conceit.

When one considers that over half of all architectural practices consist of one or two persons, and over 80 per cent have a complement of technical staff no greater than five, the disparity between the task and the resource is patently evident. During the early 1960s, this problem was recognised within the establishment of the profession, and much effort was expended on persuading small firms to merge and form larger groups or multi-disciplinary practices. The movement towards larger working groups was not successful, and though there are today a number of large and widely-skilled firms, small practices continue to proliferate.

The profession clearly likes working in small units, and there is much to be said for retaining the network of small practices where there is a personal relationship between architect and client and each architect maintains his independence and personal characteristics. On the other hand, the profession's clientele has recognised the shortcomings of the small practice, and the larger, more prestigious, and more profitable jobs are increasingly being placed with the larger multi-disciplinary practices. Nowhere is this fact better demonstrated than in the results of the liability survey carried out by the RIBA, which show that the earnings per head in the largest firms are double the average of the whole profession and three times the earnings per head in the one- and two-man practices.

All the indications are that the profession is being subjected to a squeeze, the eventual outcome of which will be a few highly prosperous, very large firms and an increasing number of small ones, struggling to exist on the smallest, least profitable, and most hazardous commissions. The downward spiral of the small practice can only be deplored, and the waste of energy and talent in the system is something to which the profession needs to apply itself urgently.

It may be time that architects re-examined their role in the building procurement process, and in particular, the title they have claimed for themselves as leaders of the building team. It is a glorious and most prestigious title, but in the present circumstances, does it really mean anything more than chief can-carrier? Is there even such a thing as a building team? In many projects, the building team is no more than a pious concept and a convenient, if misleading, label to cover all those individual participants in the building process. Without taking the team analogy too far, it would be a funny sort of football match where the goalkeeper did not arrive until half-time and the strikers left the field before the final whistle.

The architect's primary function, the one for which he has express talent and the one which he trains to exercise, is the design of buildings. If a title is required for his role, it is leader of the building *design* team. For most architects this is their involvement in the building process itself, and the administration of building contracts leads them into the most hazardous areas. For most architects, and for all but the largest firms, distancing themselves from the construction process would be the solution to many of their problems of both liability and competence. The architect's role as client's policeman and builder's safety-net is one he is often ill-equipped and always underpaid to perform, and it has contributed greatly to the builder's resignation of his own responsibilities for building properly. The sooner the architect disengages

Leader of the team

himself from site operations, the sooner will we return to proper building skills and responsibilities in the contracting trade. There are, of course, already moves in this direction in the organisation of design–build projects. In such projects, where the builder takes over responsibility for the final product, he seldom requires the architect to carry out any 'supervisory' duties at all, and who is to say that design–build projects are of any lower standard than those carried out by the conventional procurement process?

Major changes in the architect's role are probably a long way off, and in the short term we will certainly continue to practise on the basis of the service set out in the *Architect's appointment*. The range of duties and the expanse of knowledge required to fulfill the obligations of the basic service are wide indeed. Furthermore, they are changing all the time. If an architect hands a copy of the *Architect's appointment* to a client, then the client is entitled to expect that the architect is competent and able to carry out the duties set out in that document. How justified is that assumption? The truth is that nobody knows, certainly not the Institute itself that promulgates the document. Once an architect has satisfied the entry qualifications, and subject only to paying his annual subscription, the Institute has no further interest in his abilities or competence. The need for an architect to maintain and update his competence is recognised, and the Institute promotes continuing professional development (CPD) for those who wish to avail themselves of it. But there is no compulsion to do so, nor, at the present time, is there any system for monitoring the actual performance of the Institute's practising members. There are signs that this may change in the foreseeable future, although progress is slow in the face of entrenched opposition to the concept of the Institute's intruding into this area. As long ago as 1972, the council of the RIBA resolved to investigate the possibility of making the competence of its members a disciplinary issue. The investigation was stalled, ostensibly through lack of funds to carry it out. In 1982, a proposal by the education committee to investigate the possibility of making CPD mandatory was conclusively vetoed by the RIBA council. This was followed by a proposal to make the maintenance of his competence an obligation on a member under the Code of Conduct. The upshot of that proposal was yet another recommendation to the council to investigate the legal implications of such a measure, and it is probable that this time the necessary work might actually go ahead. But even if the study indicates the feasibility of the proposal, it is likely to be several years before the necessary changes are brought into effect.

The monitoring by a professional institute of the competence of its members is no easy task. This is particularly so in a profession where the activities of its members are as diffuse as in architecture. Furthermore, it has to be recognised that competence is not simply a matter of knowledge, but of knowledge and ability relevant to the particular task in hand. Clearly, it has to be recognised that the level of competence in any member, or any practice, needs to relate to the activities that are undertaken. Different skills and levels of competence are required for the design of a village hall and for a teaching hospital. It is not necessary for the designer of the former to demonstrate the skills and competence of the firm engaged on the latter.

So any investigation of the competence of members implies knowledge of both the workload and the organisation of the practice concerned. This in turn implies that the Institute will have to adopt a much more intrusive role in the affairs of its members. For some, this will be a cause of resentment and resistance, which will be overcome only by the adoption by the Institute of much a more supportive attitude towards the practices of its members. This, in my view, is long overdue in any event. The problem for most practices is their sheer inability to retain and retrieve when necessary the enormous volume of information they require to carry out even the smallest commission. The never-ending flood of new legislation, technical information, codes of practice, British Standards, components, and materials is far greater than can be controlled in any small office. It cannot be maintained in memory, nor can it even be maintained in easily retrievable form within a small office library.

Here is a major task for the Institute to undertake, not only on behalf of its members, but on its own behalf if its relevance and credibility are to be sustained in the public view. The establishment of a central computer-accessible data store of professional expertise is becoming an urgent priority. Technically, the means certainly exist, and all that is missing are the will and the financial resource. While the size of the task should not be under-estimated, modern technology, which is at the root of so many of our liability problems, also provides the means of overcoming them.

In order to achieve these changes in the profession, it is necessary as a condition precedent to get rid of the Architects' Registration Act and ARCUK.

The double standards inherent in the existence of ARCUK are no longer acceptable. Not only has it long outlived what usefulness it ever had, it is a positive deterrent to any changes or improvements in the service that architects provide to the community.

Time was, when virtually all registered architects were also members of the RIBA. Today, more than 20 per cent are content with mere registration. Any move made by the Institute to improve the performance of its members, either by raising additional funds or by increasing the stringency with which it monitors their performance, has to be weighed against the risk of losing members and income.

Under the terms of the Registration Act that brought it into existence, ARCUK is unable to perform any useful role in ensuring the competence of its members. Its only sanction is removal from the register for 'disgraceful conduct', a term related almost entirely to matters that are the subject of criminal law. The relaxed code of conduct, approved by ARCUK in 1981, provides no control or sanctions relating to quality of performance, and ARCUK has neither the funds nor the authority to pursue these matters. It has even found itself incapable of performing its primary role of protecting the use of the title 'architect', as is shown by the proliferation of unqualified cowboys passing themselves off as 'architectural consultants' — a nuance totally lost on an ignorant and gullible public.

The RIBA is the only body with the ability, authority, and will to do anything about the standards of competence and service provided by architects. The existence of the Registration Act and ARCUK severely prejudices its power to do so.

There is no legal constraint on anybody calling himself an accountant or a surveyor — but who would doubt for one moment the pre-eminence and greater repute of these entitled to call themselves 'chartered'? The reputation and credibility of the professions can safely be left in the hands of the institutes concerned. Registration is an outworn concept that today — and increasingly — is merely indicative of lower and unacceptable standards. Abolition of ARCUK would greatly strengthen the RIBA and lead to a raising of standards throughout the profession. And with raised standards, one may hope for a lessening of claims against architects and greater protection for society at large. However much I have inveighed earlier in this book against the unjust burden carried by architects, we must never forget that at the heart of many building claims is some delinquent act or omission by the architect concerned.

Even though we may seek to excuse or explain this unpalatable fact, we have a bounden duty as a profession to find ways to reduce the culpable errors we commit. The errors of the individual reflect upon the profession as a whole, and the public will be far more sympathetic to our demands for relief from our liability burdens if it can be seen that we have society's interests in mind, as well as our own.